JUVENILE DELINQUENCY IN THE UNITED STATES AND THE UNITED KINGDOM

Juvenile Delinquency in the United States and the United Kingdom

Edited by

Gary L. McDowell
Institute of United States Studies
University of London

and

Jinney S. Smith
Northwestern University

Foreword by

James Q. Wilson
University of California

First published in Great Britain 1999 by
MACMILLAN PRESS LTD
Houndmills, Basingstoke, Hampshire RG21 6XS and London
Companies and representatives throughout the world

A catalogue record for this book is available from the British Library.

ISBN 0–333–66463–9

First published in the United States of America 1999 by
ST. MARTIN'S PRESS, INC.,
Scholarly and Reference Division,
175 Fifth Avenue, New York, N.Y. 10010

ISBN 0–312–22204–1

Library of Congress Cataloging-in-Publication Data
Juvenile delinquency in the United States and the United Kingdom /
edited by Gary L. McDowell, Jinney S. Smith ; foreword by James Q.
Wilson.
p. cm.
Includes bibliographical references and index.
ISBN 0–312–22204–1 (cloth)
1. Juvenile delinquency—United States—Congresses. 2. Juvenile
delinquency—Great Britain—Congresses. I. McDowell, Gary L.,
1949– . II. Smith, Jinney S., 1971– .
HV9104.J846 1999
364.36'0973—dc21   98–43701
                                                            CIP

Selection, editorial matter and Introduction © Gary L. McDowell and Jinney S. Smith 1999
Foreword © James Q. Wilson 1999
Chapter 9 © Jinney S. Smith 1999
Afterword © Mary Tuck 1999
Chapters 1–8 © Macmillan Press Ltd 1999

This book is printed on paper suitable for recycling and made from fully managed and
sustained forest sources.

10   9   8   7   6   5   4   3   2   1
08   07   06   05   04   03   02   01   00   99

Printed and bound in Great Britain by
Antony Rowe Ltd, Chippenham, Wiltshire

In memory of Mary Tuck

Contents

Notes on Contributors

Ronald P. Corbett, Jr. has worked in corrections for 20 years and is currently Deputy Commissioner of the Massachusetts Probation Department. Dr Corbett has published widely in criminal justice journals, and has been recognized for his contributions to criminal justice by the New England Council on Crime and Delinquency (the Manson-Robinson Award in 1994) and by the American Probation and Parole Association (the Sam Houston State University Award in 1990). He is also Immediate Past-President of the National Association of Probation Executives. In addition, Dr Corbett has taught part-time for almost 20 years, and currently serves as Adjunct Professor in the graduate program at the University of Massachusetts-Lowell. In 1990, he received the William Haskell Memorial Distinguished Teaching Award from the University of Massachusetts.

David P. Farrington, FBA, is Professor of Psychological Criminology at Cambridge University, where he has been on the faculty since 1969. His major research interest is in the longitudinal study of delinquency and crime. Dr Farrington is Director of the Cambridge Study in Delinquent Development, a prospective longitudinal study of over 400 London males from age eight to age 40. He is also co-Principal Investigator of the Pittsburgh Youth Survey, a prospective longitudinal study of over 1500 males from age 7 to 18. In addition to over 150 articles on criminological and psychological topics, he has published 13 books, one of which, *Understanding and Controlling Crime* (1986), won the prize for distinguished scholarship of the American Sociological Association Criminology Section. He is a member of a number of academic and advisory boards in America, Europe and the United Kingdom, and was awarded the Sellin-Glueck Award of the American Society of Criminology for international contributions to criminology.

Lawrence A. Greenfeld is Deputy Director of the Bureau of Justice Statistics, the statistical arm of the United States

Department of Justice. Mr Greenfeld holds an MS in Administration of Justice from American University, and has been employed in local, state, and federal criminal justice agencies for nearly three decades. He has authored more than 60 publications appearing in refereed journals, government reports, and edited volumes. Mr Greenfeld has served on numerous national panels and commissions, including the Surgeon General's National Advisory Commission on Drunk Driving. His contributions to criminal justice have been recognized by awards from the American Correctional Association (the Lejins Award in 1993), and he was selected as the 'Best of the Best' in the field of corrections by *Corrections Today*.

Maureen A. Henneberg has served as the Chief of Planning, Management and Budget in the Bureau of Justice Statistics since 1991. She graduated *magna cum laude* with a BA in political science from the State University of New York-Genesseo in 1988. After receiving her Master of Public Administration (concentrating in judicial administration) from American University in 1990, Ms Henneberg spent a year at the Bureau of Justice Statistics as a Presidential Management Intern, also holding a rotational assignment at the Federal Judicial Center's Judicial Education Division.

Edwin Meese III served as United States Attorney General in the Reagan administration, and was among President Reagan's important advisors. As Chairman of the Domestic Policy Council and the National Drug Policy Board, and as a member of the National Security Council, he played a key role in the development and execution of domestic and foreign policy. During the 1970s Mr Meese was Director of the Center for Criminal Justice Policy and Management and Professor of Law at the University of San Diego. Before this he was a local prosecutor in California. He is currently the Ronald Reagan Distinguished Fellow in Public Policy at The Heritage Foundation. He also is a Distinguished Visiting Fellow at the Hoover Institution, Stanford University, and a Distinguished Senior Fellow at the Institute of United States Studies, University of London.

Patricia Morgan is a sociologist specializing in criminology and family policy, and is currently Senior Research Fellow on the Family at the Institute of Economic Affairs' Health and Welfare Unit in London. In addition to contributing frequently to television and radio programs in the UK, Ms Morgan has authored or co-authored six books, and contributed chapters to several others.

Ralph A. Rossum is the Henry Salvatori Professor of American Constitutionalism at Claremont McKenna College and a member of the faculty of Claremont Graduate University. Dr Rossum has authored five books and over 50 articles in legal and professional journals on criminal and juvenile justice topics, in addition to *American Constitutional Law*, now in its fourth edition. He has served as a member of the Board of the National Institute of Justice, and as Deputy Director of the Bureau of Justice Statistics, both in the US Department of Justice. Professor Rossum co-directed the conference on comparative juvenile justice at the University of London in 1994 that gave rise to this edited volume.

Andrew Rutherford is currently Professor of Law and Criminal Policy at Southampton University in the Faculty of Law, where he has been since 1979. After graduating from Durham University and Cambridge University, Professor Rutherford worked as an assistant and later deputy governor of the Prison Service between 1962 and 1973. During 1968–70 and 1973–9 he studied, researched or taught in the US at the University of California, Yale Law School, Ohio State University, University of Minnesota and at Abt Associates in Massachusetts. Professor Rutherford is actively involved with the Howard League for Penal Reform and has served as its chairman since 1984. Between 1994 and 1996 he was a member of the National Criminal Justice Commission in the United States. He has authored four books, and edited two others, in the area of criminal justice and policy.

Jonathan Sacks has been Chief Rabbi of the United Hebrew Congregations of the Commonwealth since 1991, and is the sixth rabbi to hold this office since 1845. Previously Dr Sacks had been the Principal of Jews' College, London, the world's oldest rabbinical seminary, where he also held the Chair in Modern Jewish Thought. The Chief Rabbi is a frequent contributor to radio, television, and the national British press, and has authored 11 books. In addition, he has held several distinguished visiting professorships and lectureships at universities throughout Great Britain, including Manchester University, Newcastle University and the Universities of Oxford, Essex, Edinburgh and St Andrews.

Jinney S. Smith is currently a Ph.D. candidate in the Department of Political Science at Northwestern University, Evanston, Illinois. She received her BA in political science and history with high honors from the University of Michigan-Ann Arbor in 1992, and her MS in criminal justice from Northeastern University in 1993. Before beginning her doctoral studies, Ms Smith worked as research assistant on criminal justice projects at Northeastern University and Harvard University (at Radcliffe College and the John F. Kennedy School of Government). Ms Smith gratefully acknowledges the support of the Institute of United States Studies which allowed her to complete an earlier version of this chapter that was presented at the 'Democracy and Justice: Reviewing Crime in Theory and Practice Conference' held at Brunel University, England, in June 1995.

Mary Tuck, CBE, was the Head of the Home Office Research and Planning Unit from 1984 until her retirement in 1990, where she was responsible for innovative research in the area of criminology. A former Fulbright Fellow in the United States, Mrs Tuck was a journalist, researcher, and academic before joining the British Civil Service in 1975. Her publications include studies on youth crime and crime in the inner cities. After her retirement, Mrs Tuck was active in the field of criminal justice through her involvement in the Economic and Social Research Council, the Parole Board, the Lord Chancellor's Advisory Committee on Legal Education and as National Chair of Victim Support. She passed away on 20 October 1996.

Foreword

James Q. Wilson

Professor of Management and Public Policy,
University of California, Los Angeles

The dramatic increase in property crime that has occurred since the late 1950s or early 1960s in North America and much of Europe has led many people to wonder what has happened to societies that, apparently, have been unable to convert rising material prosperity and greater human freedom into a decent social order. We earn more money; we enjoy more opportunities; and we steal more.

The nations that have experienced this rise in crime have quite different political and crime control strategies. These differences help explain, I think, why crime rates have not risen at exactly the same rate everywhere and why, in some cases, there have been recent decreases in crime in some nations while the increases have continued in others. But the different rates at which people are arrested, prosecuted, convicted, and punished, though important, do not explain why the great increase in crime, whatever its local variations, has been so widespread, extending, in so far as we can tell, across almost all industrialized democracies.

This general increase has led many people to wonder whether Western nations have somehow lost the capacity to socialize their young people. In their chapter on American data, Lawrence A. Greenfeld and Maureen A. Henneberg show that the number of arrests for violent crimes for every 100 000 persons aged 15 to 20 increased by over 45 per cent between those born in 1963 and those born in 1976. The heightened criminality of children born in recent years is confirmed by looking at the prior arrests for violent crimes among the inmates of American state prisons. Only about five per cent of the inmates born in 1959 had a prior violent juvenile arrest, but among those born in 1972 over 15 per cent had such a record. Much the same lesson has been learned from Professor Marvin Wolfgang and his colleagues at the

University of Pennsylvania. When they compared the criminal careers of the boys born in Philadelphia in 1945 with those born there in 1958, they found that the latter group committed more serious crimes.

David Farrington suggests that much the same story is probably true in Great Britain. Though some people claim that there has been a decline in British juvenile offending, what really changed was not how many youngsters got in trouble with the law, but how they were counted. Since the mid-1980s, police officers have begun issuing unrecorded warnings to juvenile offenders rather than, as in the past, recorded ones, and the Crown Prosecution Service refused to prosecute many young offenders unless their crimes were serious or they were caught repeatedly. As a result, it only appears that the juvenile offense rate has declined.

None of these findings will surprise the average reader. Most of them believe that something is wrong with any society that, in the midst of rising prosperity, allows more and more young people to become hardened criminals. Both David Farrington and Ralph Rossum summarize what we know about the origins of serious young offenders. The story is depressing. Young criminals come disproportionately from weak, abusive, neglectful, or criminal families. Serious crime is not a skill learned by adults, it is a habit acquired by children.

The proportion of such families has been rising. In the United States and in much of Western Europe there has been a steady increase in the number of children born out of wedlock and raised by single parents. The best scholarly studies of single-parent families done in the United States show that children raised in mother-only families are more likely than those raised in two-parent ones to be suspended from school, to display emotional problems, and to behave badly – even after controlling for family income and ethnicity. Patricia Morgan in her essay develops this point with skill and power.

What families give to children is their character. Good families help their children acquire self-control and a reasonable concern for the welfare of others. Bad families, by their own neglect, abusiveness, or criminality, help their children learn self-indulgence and a desire to take advantage of others. Bad two-parent families are ones in which the mother and father fight constantly, get drunk or take drugs, are episodically employed, and are cruel or inconsistent in raising children. Bad one-parent families are ones in which the mother cannot cope with child-rearing, lacks the education necessary to get and hold a job, farms the child out to the care of others, and indulges in drinking and drug abuse.

Hardly anyone needs to be persuaded of these connections. Bad families have always existed and worked their mischief; in earlier centuries they were probably more common than they are now. But today we expect more than we have received from family life. We expect it because in most industrialized nations life-threatening poverty has been all but eliminated, the conditions of work have been made relatively safe and well-paid, and the police are a reasonably neutral public agency and not the arm of a self-aggrandizing warlord. Family life was difficult when life was short, money scarce, and freedom absent; why has it become difficult for some people now that life is long, money available, and freedom everywhere?

Perhaps because of these very changes. When people are emancipated from feudal power, industrial drudgery, and political tyranny, most of them use their freedom wisely to invent new ideas, start new businesses, and enjoy a fuller life. But some find freedom menacing. The controls of village and church life that once checked their extravagances and directed their energies are gone, replaced only with such direction as can be supplied by an unsteady temperament and a desire for self-indulgence. When such people are placed in large cities, they find themselves in neighborhoods made up in part of people with similar moods who have access to opportunities for giving them expression. Drugs are sold openly, liquor stores abound on every street corner, guns are readily available, and gangs become substitutes for families.

Perhaps, in short, it is our progress that has created our problems. This is especially likely if the cultural and political elites choose to emphasize personal liberation and economic consumption. As Jonathan Sacks points out, the desire for personal freedom and weakly constrained consumption was given an eloquent defense by John Stuart Mill in his book, *On Liberty*. My experience as a college professor convinced me that most students, and certainly the largest share of the best students, are libertarians as Mill hoped they would be. The law should not constrain us, he argued, save to prevent us from harming others. Rabbi Sacks, in his penetrating essay, takes a different view. To him, the law cannot simply abandon control of private behavior unless it supports those institutions – chiefly families, schools, and religious organizations – that will produce a restraint on private behavior equivalent to what the law once produced.

This view does not commend itself to many leaders except as a verbal formulation designed to give expression to a loose concern for human decency. To them, a free society is, almost by definition, one that cannot use private entities to shape character. To them, character is the product of self-discovery, not external tutelage. This view is wrong and embracing it is mistaken, as is evident in the political desire to protect biological parents however badly they treat their children, to convert schools into instruments of wholly technical education devoid of much moral content, and to create (at least in the United States) nearly insuperable barriers to the use of public funds for the non-discriminatory support of religious organizations.

But if we desire personal freedom and reject moral education, all that is left to constrain juvenile offenders is the weak reed of juvenile courts. Ralph Rossum suggests that this reed is not only weak, but already broken. Ronald Corbett, Jr., offers some suggestions for changing a weak reed into a strong force, but it remains to be seen whether any of this will work. The juvenile court, after all, was designed to handle children in need of supervision, not children who had robbed, raped, or killed. It was based on the assumption that it would supply parental guidance in those few cases where such guidance was not already available from real parents. Today, a juvenile judge who summons the parents of a troubled child to court is likely to find not two parents but, at most, one, and that one so disturbed by drugs or alcohol as to be useless in discharging the tasks the judge wishes to impose.

The problem to which this book is addressed is far more serious than is implied by the title, *Juvenile Delinquency in the*

United States and United Kingdom. The book is really about the central problem of a modern industrial society: how can one enjoy the benefits of personal emancipation while retaining the moral instruction of a coherent social order? No-one has yet discovered the answer.

Preface and Acknowledgments

In February 1993 a toddler named Jamie Bulger was taken from his mother's side in a shopping mall near Liverpool, marched a mile or so down the road to a railway track and brutally murdered. Even a world grown used to violence was shaken by the event. But what was especially shocking was that his killers were two ten-year-old boys, Robert Thompson and Jon Venables. As their smiling schoolday photographs appeared on the front pages of newspapers everywhere, people groped for answers as to how such a thing could occur. Many could only conclude, as Chief Rabbi Dr Jonathan Sacks wrote in *The Times*, that the 'moral fabric with which we clothe our children has grown threadbare. The holes have begun to show.'

This collection of essays grew from a conference that was held at the Institute of United States Studies in the University of London in the wake of the murder of Jamie Bulger and the subsequent conviction of Robert Thompson and Jon Venables. The purpose of that meeting, 'Juvenile Justice and the Limits of Social Policy', was to assemble experts from the United States and the United Kingdom in order to explore the common ground the two nations share. The topics covered ranged from the technical and the procedural to considerations of moral judgment, the erosion of the family and the influence on children of violent video films in the home. In the end, much of the discussion came to focus on the question of character and how best to educate children in order to develop their moral sensibility.

A great many people contributed to the planning of the conference, but special thanks must go to David Faulkner, a Senior Research Associate at the University of Oxford Centre for Criminological Research, and to the late Mary Tuck, formerly Head of Research at the Home Office. Their counsel and suggestions made the meeting a far richer one where it concerned the British experience than it otherwise would have been. The guidance of

Ralph Rossum and former Attorney General Edwin Meese III similarly meant that proper attention was paid to the American side. Anna Brooke lent her superb organizational and administrative skills throughout.

Over two dozen practitioners, scholars, and political figures addressed the conference, and we present here a cross-section of papers representing the significant and recurring issues which were raised and debated. We thank all the authors for their excellent essays, but particular thanks go to Ronald Corbett, who did not attend the conference and who wrote an original paper. Jonathan Sacks' chapter, upon which his conference remarks were based, is taken from his book *Faith in the Future*, published and copyright 1995 by Darton, Longman and Todd Ltd., and used by permission of the publishers. We also gratefully acknowledge the help of several individuals in preparing this volume for publication. Lucy Pratt, of the Institute of United States Studies, provided research assistance and managed smoothly what otherwise would have been a chaotic process of co-ordinating authors and editors across the Atlantic. Christina Zaba, our editorial services controller at Macmillan, skillfully copy-edited the manuscript and shepherded it through Macmillan's production process with great efficiency. Without the support of Tim Farmiloe, our commissioning editor at Macmillan, this book simply would not exist.

Although many people donated countless hours to both the conference and this volume, neither would have been possible without the support of the John M. Olin Foundation of New York. We are especially grateful to the foundation for their support, moral as well as financial.

We dedicate this book to the late Mary Tuck, who passed away on 20 October 1996, in tribute to her long and distinguished public service and academic careers in the areas of criminal justice administration and criminology. Presented as the Afterword is an early, but substantively complete, draft of the chapter she was preparing for this volume before her untimely death.

Gary L. McDowell
Jinney S. Smith

Part I
The Crisis of Delinquency

1 Predicting Persistent Young Offenders

David P. Farrington

POLICY ISSUES

In the United Kingdom in the 1990s, there has been a great deal of concern with persistent young offenders. This has arisen partly because a large increase in crime in the 1980s – and especially in the types of crimes particularly committed by young people, such as burglary and taking vehicles – coincided with a decrease in the number of recorded juvenile offenders. Because crime was increasing while the prevalence of juvenile offending was decreasing, it was argued, the average juvenile offender must be committing more crimes. Hence, there was the perception that the number of persistent young offenders – as opposed to young offenders in general – was increasing.

Unfortunately, there is no evidence of a disproportional increase in the number of persistent young offenders. Yet the increase in crime is unquestionable. For example, between 1981 and 1991 the number of burglaries in England and Wales increased by 82 per cent according to the British Crime Survey, and by 70 per cent according to national police statistics; and the number of vehicle thefts increased by 81 per cent according to the British Crime Survey and by 75 per cent according to national police statistics (Farrington *et al.*, 1994). The decrease in recorded juvenile offenders is also unquestionable. For example, the rate of recorded offenders (convictions plus cautions for indictable offences) of males increased from 50 per 1000 in 1981 to 55 per 1000 in 1985, but then decreased by one third to only 37 per 1000 in 1989 (Farrington, 1992b).

Unfortunately, it is highly unlikely that the decrease in recorded juvenile offenders coincided with a true decrease in the number of juvenile offenders. The reasons for the recorded decrease almost

3

certainly lie in procedural changes. Beginning in the mid-1980s, police forces began to issue unrecorded warnings to apprehended juvenile offenders rather than recorded cautions (Farrington, 1992b). Another contributory factor to the recorded decrease was the creation of the Crown Prosecution Service in 1986, which transferred responsibility for prosecuting offenders from the police to lawyers. For example, the number of recorded juvenile shoplifters decreased by half between 1985 and 1990, whereas the number of juvenile shoplifters apprehended by retailers did not decrease (Farrington and Burrows, 1993). Retailers stated that they had been told not to report shoplifters to the police because the Crown Prosecution Service would not prosecute juveniles unless the value of stolen property was high or they were caught repeatedly. Another factor was the Police and Criminal Evidence Act 1984, which increased procedural safe-guards for alleged offenders and hence made it easier for true offenders to escape justice (Irving and McKenzie, 1989).

For all these reasons, it is very likely that the dramatic increase in crime between 1981 and 1991 coincided with a true increase in the number of juvenile offenders. The number of recorded juvenile offenders only decreased because the probability of being convicted or cautioned after offending decreased. Life got better for juvenile offenders. There may well have been an increase in persistent juvenile offenders in proportion to the increase in juvenile offenders in general, but it is unlikely that the total increase in juvenile crime was entirely or predominantly attributable to an increase in persistent juvenile offenders.

Another reason for an increased political concern and mass media interest in young offenders in the 1990s was the James Bulger murder in 1993, which shocked the nation. Two boys aged about 11 abducted and murdered a toddler. Unfortunately, this dramatic increase in public concern only served to highlight the lack of up-to-date knowledge about juvenile crime. Suddenly, there was great interest in the causes of juvenile crime, but hardly any fundamental research on this topic had been funded by the British government for many years. Because of this, it was not possible for public discussions about juvenile crime in the 1990s to be informed by modern British research on its causes.

The mass-media panic about juvenile crime spurred the Home Office into hastily commissioning some research on persistent young offenders (Hagell and Newburn, 1994); my understanding is that the researchers were told that they had to produce a report within 8 months of beginning. Obviously, it is not ideal for research to be conducted under such extreme pressure of time.

Another reason for the increased concern with young offenders in the 1990s was the fact that very few offenders under the age of 15 were being sent to institutions. This was only possible for cases which fell within Section 53 of the Children and Young Persons Act 1933, which covered very serious offenses (Boswell, 1995). The mass media delighted in focusing on cases such as persistent young offenders placed under the care of the social services who were sent on a holiday to Egypt or Spain, or who were sent to a holiday camp and then burgled the chalets. Consequently, the Government introduced Secure Training Orders for offenders aged 12 to 14 in the Criminal Justice and Public Order Act 1994. The minimum qualification for such an order was being convicted on three separate occasions.

THEORETICAL ISSUES

A great deal is known from classic longitudinal studies about the characteristics of young offenders. The typical delinquent – a male property offender – tends to be born in a low-income, large-sized family and to have criminal parents. When he is young, his parents supervise him rather poorly, use harsh or erratic child-rearing techniques, and are likely to be in conflict and to separate. At school, he tends to have low intelligence and attainment, is troublesome, hyperactive, and impulsive, and often truants. He tends to associate with friends who are also delinquents.

After leaving school, the typical delinquent tends to have a low-status job record punctuated by periods of unemployment. His deviant behavior tends to be versatile rather than specialized. He not only commits property offenses such as theft and burglary, but also engages in violence, vandalism, drug use, excessive drinking, reckless driving, and sexual promiscuity. His likelihood of offending reaches a peak during his teenage years and then declines in his twenties, when he is likely to get married or cohabit with a woman.

While a great deal is known about differences between young offenders and non-offenders, far less is known about whether persistent young offenders are qualitatively or quantitatively different from other (that is, occasional) young offenders. Generally, delinquency theories aim to explain differences between offenders and non-offenders rather than between persistent and occasional offenders. While this discussion focuses on official delinquents, predictors and correlates of official delinquency are generally similar to predictors and correlates of self-reported delinquency (Farrington, 1992a). However, the cut-off point between persistent and occasional offenders would obviously be different for self-reported delinquency.

Several researchers, such as LeBlanc and Frechette (1989) in Canada, and Moffitt (1993) in the United States, have distinguished between two different categories of offenders. On the one hand there are occasional, opportunistic, uncommitted offenders who have relatively short criminal careers, perhaps limited to their teenage years, heavily influenced by their peers and often motivated by excitement-seeking. On the other hand, there are more persistent, committed offenders with much longer criminal careers, often extending from childhood into adulthood, more versatile in their offending patterns and more rationally motivated in their offending.

A key issue is how far persistent offenders are merely more extreme cases than occasional offenders, rather than being qualitatively different. This would certainly be the argument of Gottfredson and Hirschi (1990): persistent offenders just have lower self-control than occasional offenders. However, proponents of the criminal career approach, such as Blumstein *et al.* (1988), would argue that factors influencing the onset of offending may be different from factors influencing the persistence of offending after onset. Hence, differences between offenders and non-offenders may not be the same as differences between persistent and occasional offenders.

The latest Green Paper from the Home Office (1997) seemed to argue in favor of the second idea. In paragraph 30, it asserts that 'the personalities of many young offenders are indistinguishable from those of non-offenders', and goes on to emphasize the importance of family, school, and peer influences on offending. However, it also states that persistent and serious offenders are different in personality factors such as aggressiveness, dishonesty, cruelty, impulsiveness, and selfishness.

The main aim of this chapter is to investigate the predictors of persistent and occasional young offenders, compared with non-offenders, in the Cambridge Study in Delinquent Development. The key questions are the following:

1. What factors predict offending compared with non-offending?
2. What factors predict persistent offending compared with occasional offending?
3. What factors predict occasional offending compared with non-offending?

THE CAMBRIDGE STUDY IN DELINQUENT DEVELOPMENT

The Cambridge Study in Delinquent Development is a prospective longitudinal survey of the development of offending and anti-social behavior in 411 London males. At the time they were first contacted in 1961–2, these males were all living in a working-class inner-city area of South London. The sample was chosen by taking all the boys who were then aged 8 or 9 and on the registers of six state primary schools within a one-mile radius of a research office that had been established. The most common year of birth of these males was therefore 1953. In nearly all cases (94 per cent), their family breadwinner at that time (usually the father) had a working-class occupation (skilled, semi-skilled, or unskilled manual worker). Most of the boys were white (97 per cent) and of British origin. The study was originally directed by Donald J. West, and it has been directed since 1982 by David P. Farrington, who has worked on it since 1969. It has been mainly funded by the Home Office. The major results can be found in four books (West, 1969, 1982; West and Farrington, 1973, 1977), in more than 60 papers listed by Farrington and West (1990), and in a summary paper by Farrington (1995). These publications should be consulted for more details about the variables measured in this chapter.

The original aim of the Study was to describe the development of delinquent and criminal behavior in inner-city males, to investigate how far it could be predicted in advance, and to explain why juvenile delinquency began, why it did or did not continue into adult crime, and why adult crime usually ended as men reached their twenties. The main focus was on continuity or discontinuity in behavioral development, on the effects of life events on development, and on predicting future behavior. The study was not designed to test any one particular theory about delinquency but to test many different hypotheses about the causes and correlates of offending. One reason for casting the net wide at the start and measuring many different variables was the belief that theoretical fashions changed over time and that it was important to try to measure as many variables as possible in which future researchers might be interested. Another reason for measuring a wide range of variables was the fact that long-term longitudinal surveys are very uncommon, and that the value of this particular one would be enhanced if it yielded information of use not only to delinquency researchers but also to those interested in alcohol and drug use, educational difficulties, poverty and poor housing, unemployment, sexual behavior, aggression, other social problems, and human development generally.

A major aim in this survey, therefore, was to measure as many factors as possible that were alleged to be causes or correlates of offending. The males were interviewed and tested in their schools when they were aged about 8, 10, and 14, by male or female psychologists. They were interviewed in a research office at about 16, 18, and 21, and in their homes at about 25 and 32, by young male social science graduates. At all ages except 21 and 25 the aim was to interview the whole sample, and it was always possible to trace and interview a high proportion: 389 out of the 410 who were still alive at age 18 (95 per cent) and 378 out of the 403 who were still alive at age 32 (94 per cent), for example. The tests in schools measured individual characteristics such as intelligence, attainment, personality, and psychomotor impulsivity, while information was collected in the interviews about such topics as living circumstances, employment histories, relationships with females, leisure activities such as drinking and fighting, and offending behavior.

In addition to interviews and tests with the males, interviews with their parents were carried out by female social workers who visited their homes. These took place about once a year from when the boy was about 8 until when he was aged between 14 and 15 and was in his last year of compulsory education. The primary informant was the mother, although many fathers were also seen. The parents provided details about such matters as family income, family size, their employment histories, their child-rearing practices (including attitudes, discipline, and parental disharmony), their degree of supervision of the boy, and his temporary or permanent separations from them. Also, when the boy was aged 12, the parents completed questionnaires about their child-rearing attitudes and about his leisure activities.

The teachers completed questionnaires when the boys were aged about 8, 10, 12, and 14. These furnished data about their troublesome and aggressive school behavior, their attention deficits, their school attainments, and their truancy. Ratings were also obtained from their peers when they were in the primary schools, about such topics as their daring, dishonesty, troublesomeness, and popularity.

Searches were also carried out in the central Criminal Record Office (National Identification Service) in London to try to locate findings of guilt of the males, of their parents, of their brothers and sisters, and (in recent years) of their wives and cohabitees. The minimum age of criminal responsibility in England is 10. The Criminal Record Office contains records of all relatively serious offenses committed in Great Britain or Ireland, and also acts as a repository for records of minor juvenile offenses committed in London. In the case of 18 males who had emigrated outside Great Britain and Ireland by age 32, applications were made to search their criminal records in the eight countries where they had settled, and searches were actually carried out in four countries. Since most males did not emigrate until their twenties, and since the emigrants had rarely been convicted in England, it is likely that the criminal records are quite complete.

The latest search of conviction records took place in the summer of 1994, when most of the males were aged 40. Up to that time, 164 males (40 per cent) were convicted (Farrington *et al.*, 1996). In this chapter, the recorded age of offending is the age at which an offense was committed, not the age at conviction. There can be delays of several months or even more than a year between offenses and convictions, making conviction ages different from offending ages. Offenses are defined as acts leading to convictions, and only offenses committed on different days were counted. Where two or more offenses were committed on the same day, only the most serious one was counted. Most court appearances arose from only one offending day; the 760 recorded offenses up to age 40 corresponded to 686 separate occasions of conviction.

Convictions were only counted if they were for offenses normally recorded in the Criminal Record Office, thereby excluding minor crimes such as common assault, traffic infractions, and drunkenness. The most common offenses included were thefts, burglaries, and unauthorized takings of vehicles, although there were also quite a few offenses of violence, vandalism, fraud, and drug abuse. In order not to rely on official records for information about offending, self-reports of offending were obtained from the males at every age from 14 to 32.

For the present analyses each variable was dichotomized, as far as possible, into the 'worst' quarter of males (e.g. the quarter with lowest income or lowest intelligence) versus the remainder. This was done in order to compare the importance of different variables and also to permit a 'risk-factor' approach. Because most variables were originally classified into a small number of categories, and because fine distinctions between categories could not be made very accurately, this dichotomizing did not usually involve a great loss of information. The one-quarter/ three-quarters split was chosen to match the prior expectation that about one-quarter of the sample would be convicted as juveniles. Variables were not included in the analysis if more than about 10 per cent of the sample were not known on them.

The Cambridge Study in Delinquent Development has a unique combination of features:

1. Eight personal interviews with the males have been completed over a period of 24 years, from age 8 to 32;
2. The main focus of interest is on offending, which has been studied from age 10 to 40;
3. The sample size of about 400 is large enough for many statistical analyses but small enough to permit detailed case histories of the boys and their families;
4. There has been a very low attrition rate, since 94 per cent of the males still alive provided information at age 32;
5. Information has been obtained from multiple sources: the males, their parents, teachers, peers, and official records;
6. Information has been obtained about a wide variety of theoretical constructs, including intelligence, personality, parental child-rearing methods, peer delinquency, school behavior, employment success, marital stability, and so on.

Persistent Young Offenders and Childhood Troublesomeness

This chapter focuses on offenses committed between the ages of 10 and 18 inclusive and leading to convictions. In the Cambridge Study, 300 boys had no convictions, 66 had one or two convictions (the occasional offenders), and 45 had three or more convictions (the persistent offenders) between these ages. The 45 persistent offenders amassed a total of 262 convictions, or an average of 5.8 each. It might be argued that being convicted three times is not very good evidence of persistent offending, although this was the minimum criterion set for a Secure Training Order. It must be admitted that the criterion was chosen partly for analytic purposes. For example, requiring six or more convictions (a criterion previously used to identify chronic offenders up to age 25) would have identified only 21 boys – too few to draw general conclusions about characteristics of persistent offenders.

The ability of key childhood factors (measured at age 8 to 10) to predict persistent and occasional offenders, compared with non-offenders, was then studied. For example, Table 1.1 shows the relationship between troublesomeness (rated by peers and teachers) and youthful offending. Nearly two-thirds (64.4 per cent) of the persistent offenders had been rated as troublesome, compared with just over a quarter (28.8 per cent) of the occasional offenders, and one in seven (14.7 per cent) of the non-offenders. These are retrospective rather than prospective percentages, but they graphically illustrate the relationship between troublesomeness and youthful offending.

In order to measure the strength of relationships, odds ratios were calculated in 2×2 tables. Some advantages of the odds ratio are that it is not affected by sample size (unlike chi-squared, for example), nor by the prevalence of predictors or outcomes (unlike the phi correlation, for example), nor by the study design (prospective or retrospective: see Fleiss, 1981). It is easily understandable as the increase in risk associated with a risk factor, and is a more realistic measure of predictive efficiency than the percentage of variance explained (Rosenthal and Rubin, 1982). For example, an odds ratio of two, doubling the risk of delinquency, might correspond to a correlation of about 0.12, which translates into 1.4 per cent of the variance explained. The percentage of variance explained gives a misleading impression of weak relationships and low predictability.

Three odds ratios were calculated. The first measured the strength of the relationship between troublesomeness and offenders compared to non-offenders. The second measured the strength of the relationship with occasional offenders compared to non offenders, and the third measured the strength of the relationship with persistent offenders compared to occasional offenders. The other possible comparisons, between persistent offenders and non-offenders, and between persistent offenders and the remainder are less interesting. The most interesting question is: Given a difference between offenders and non-offenders, is there also a difference between occasional offenders and non-offenders, between persistent offenders and occasional offenders, or in both cases?

As an example, consider the relationship between troublesomeness and persistent versus occasional offenders. Note that this comparison is only based on 111 boys, whereas the comparison between offenders and non-offenders is based on 411 boys.

This is why it is essential to use a measure of strength of relationship that is not affected by sample size. The odds of being persistent for troublesome boys is 29/19 (1.53), whereas the odds of being persistent for non-troublesome boys is 16/47 (0.34). Hence, the odds ratio (OR) is 4.5 (1.53 divided by 0.34), a very strong relationship compared to the chance value of 1.0. This OR was statistically significant; one-tailed tests were used because all predictions were directional (e.g. in this case, it is predicted that troublesome boys are more delinquent and more persistent).

Troublesomeness also significantly predicted offenders compared with non-offenders (OR = 4.4) and occasional offenders compared with non-offenders (OR = 2.4). As a rule of thumb, an OR of two or greater, doubling the risk of the outcome, indicates a strong relationship. Hence, troublesomeness differentiated both between persistent and occasional offenders and between occasional offenders and non-offenders. This is not surprising, as troublesomeness is arguably measuring the same underlying theoretical construct (an antisocial personality) as offending.

The relationship between troublesomeness and offending gives a good indication of how far persistent or occasional offending could have been predicted at age 8 to 10. Looking backwards, two-thirds of the eventual persistent offenders were notably badly behaved in childhood. Looking forwards, half of the troublesome boys were not convicted.

Predicting Persistent Young Offenders

Table 1.2 shows how far 20 key childhood predictors of offending in the Cambridge Study were related to persistent and occasional offending. For example, half (51.1 per cent) of the persistent offenders came from low-income families, compared with a quarter (25.8 per cent) of the occasional offenders and one in six (17.7 per cent) of the non-offenders. Low family income significantly discriminated between persistent and occasional offenders (OR = 3.0) but not between occasional offenders and non-offenders (OR = 1.6). The same was true of low social class, coded on the Registrar General's scale according to the occupational prestige of the family breadwinner. However, poor (dilapidated or slum) housing and large family size (four or more siblings up to the tenth birthday) discriminated between occasional offenders and non-offenders, but not between persistent and occasional offenders.

The strongest predictor of offending between the ages of 10 and 18 was having a convicted parent up to the tenth birthday (OR = 4.5). However, a convicted parent discriminated strongly between occasional offenders and non-offenders (OR = 4.6) but not between persistent and occasional offenders (OR = 1.0). In criminal career terms, it might be suggested that a convicted parent influences the onset of offending (why boys start) but not persistence after onset.

The reverse relationship is seen for boys with a delinquent sibling up to the tenth birthday. Having a delinquent sibling predicts persistent compared with occasional offenders (OR = 3.6) but not occasional offenders compared with non-offenders (OR = 1.7). Again, in criminal career terms, it might be suggested that delinquent siblings influence persistence after onset rather than the onset of offending. It is plausible that parental influence should be relatively more important at an early age, and that the influence of siblings becomes more important later, in the teenage years.

A young mother (a mother who had her first child when she was a teenager) predicted offending but did not particularly discriminate between persistent and occasional offenders. More interestingly, poor child-rearing (harsh or erratic attitude or discipline), poor supervision (monitoring) and separation from a parent (usually the father, up to the tenth birthday) all discriminated between occasional offenders and non-offenders but not between persistent and occasional offenders. It is plausible that these parental factors would influence onset rather than persistence. However, surprisingly, having a father who did not join in the boy's leisure activities predicted persistence.

Attending a school with a high delinquency rate was related to both persistent and occasional offending, as was low junior school attainment (in Arithmetic, English and Verbal Reasoning tests). Conversely, low non-verbal IQ (90 or less on the Progressive Matrices test) and peer-rated unpopularity predicted offending in general but did not particularly discriminate occasional offenders from non-offenders or persistent from occasional offenders.

Poor concentration or restlessness (rated by teachers) and high impulsiveness on psychomotor tests both especially discriminated between persistent and occasional offenders. However, daring or risk-taking (rated by peers and parents) and dishonesty (rated by peers) both especially discriminated between occasional offenders and non-offenders. Finally, as already mentioned, troublesomeness predicted both persistent and occasional offending.

Multivariate Analyses

Regression analyses were carried out to investigate the most important independent predictors of (a) offenders versus non-offenders, (b) occasional offenders versus non-offenders, and (c) persistent versus occasional offenders. Strictly speaking, logistic regression analysis should be carried out with dichotomous data. However, the major problem with logistic regression is that a case that is missing on any one variable has to be deleted from the whole analysis, causing a considerable loss of data. Fortunately, with dichotomous data, ordinary least squares (OLS) regression produces very similar results to logistic regression (Cleary and Angel, 1984), and indeed, the results obtained by the two methods are mathematically related (Schlesselman, 1982, p. 245). Missing data are not such a problem with OLS regression, because missing cases can be deleted variable by variable, thereby using as much of the data as possible. Both regression methods were used in this analysis; the most important predictors are those identified by both methods.

Dishonesty and troublesomeness were not included in the analyses because they probably measure the same underlying construct as offending. Amdur (1989) pointed out that a common fault in much delinquency research was to include indicators of the outcome variable (e.g. having delinquent peers) as 'predictors' of delinquency.

Table 1.3 shows the results of the regression analyses. Because of the very small numbers in the persistent-occasional comparison (which greatly affects significance tests), *p*-values a little greater than 0.1 are shown in Table 1.3. The most important independent predictors of offenders versus non-offenders were having a convicted parent, daring, and low school attainment. Other predictors identified in one or both analyses were poor housing, a delinquent sibling, unpopularity, attending a delinquent school and large family size. In previous regression analyses carried out in the Cambridge Study (e.g. Farrington, 1990, 1993), it has been argued that the most important predictors of offending fall into five main categories: (1) socio-economic deprivation (e.g. poor housing, large family size); (2) poor parenting (e.g. poor child rearing); (3) an antisocial family (e.g. a convicted parent, a delinquent sibling); (4) school problems (e.g. low attainment, a delinquent school); and (5) hyperactivity-impulsivity-attention deficit (e.g. daring).

Interestingly, there was no overlap between the most important independent predictors of occasional offenders (versus non-offenders) and persistent offenders (versus occasional offenders). A convicted parent, daring, unpopularity, poor housing, and poor child-rearing were the most important independent predictors of occasional offending versus non-offending. Low family income, low social class, poor concentration/restlessness, psychomotor impulsivity, a delinquent sibling, and a father who did not join in the boy's leisure activities were the most important independent predictors of persistent versus occasional offending.

DISCUSSION AND CONCLUSIONS

The fact that the predictors of persistent offending are different from the predictors of occasional offending is concordant with previous research in the Cambridge Study. For example, Farrington and Hawkins (1991) found that the most important non-behavioral predictors of conviction between ages 10 and 20 were a convicted parent, daring, low attainment, a delinquent sibling, poor child-rearing, and poor housing, whereas the most important predictors of reconviction between the ages of 21 and 32 (among those previously convicted) included some factors measured at age 8 to 10 (the father not joining in the boy's leisure activities, low verbal IQ) and some later factors (unemployment at 16, heavy drinking at 18). Farrington and West (1993) found that the most important non-behavioral predictors of conviction up to age 32 were a convicted parent, daring, low attainment, poor housing, separation from a parent, and large family size, whereas the most important predictors of chronic versus non-chronic offenders were a delinquent sibling, poor concentration/restlessness, low parental interest in education, daring, and low social class. (For earlier related analyses, see Blumstein *et al.*, 1985; Farrington, 1987.)

Similar results were obtained in the present analyses. It is tempting to conclude that a convicted parent, daring, unpopularity, poor housing and poor child-rearing are somehow implicated in the onset of offending, whereas low family income, low social class, poor concentration/restlessness, psychomotor impulsivity, a delinquent sibling, and a father who does not join in the boy's leisure activities are somehow implicated in explaining persistence after onset. These results suggest that delinquency theories need to be more specific, aiming to explain onset and persistence separately. Similarly, policy-oriented research on youthful offending needs to take account of the fact that the predictors of persistence are different from the predictors of offending in general. Finally, persistent young offenders can be identified to a considerable extent between the ages of 8 and 10.

Table 1.1   Troublesomeness at 8–10 *vs.* Convictions at 10–18

	No. Convictions			Total
	None	Occasional (1, 2)	Persistent (3+)	
Troublesome	44	19	29	92
(%)	(14.7)	(28.8)	(64.4)	(22.4)
Not troublesome	256	47	16	319
Total	300	66	45	411

Odds Ratio (Offender *vs.* Non-Offender) = 4.4
Odds Ratio (Occasional *vs.* Non-Offender) = 2.4
Odds Ratio (Persistent *vs.* Occasional) = 4.5

Table 1.2   Predicting Persistent Young Offenders

Factors at 8–10	Percent of			Odds Ratios		
	None	Occ.	Pers.	None vs. Del.	None vs. Occ.	Occ. vs. Pers.
Low family income	17.7	25.8	51.1	2.6*	1.6	3.0*
Poor housing	31.3	50.0	53.3	2.3*	2.2*	1.1
Low social class	17.0	18.2	35.6	1.6*	1.1	2.5*
Large family size	18.3	36.4	44.4	2.9*	2.5*	1.4
Convicted parent	18.0	50.0	48.9	4.5*	4.6*	1.0
Delinquent sibling	7.7	12.1	33.3	3.1*	1.7	3.6*
Young mother	19.0	27.3	37.8	2.0*	1.6	1.6
Poor child rearing	19.5	31.7	46.3	2.5*	1.9*	1.9
Poor supervision	14.8	29.5	35.9	2.7*	2.4*	1.3
Father uninvolved	25.2	26.0	51.9	1.6	1.0	3.1*
Separated from parent	17.7	30.3	37.8	2.3*	2.0*	1.4
Delinquent school	15.1	28.1	46.3	3.1*	2.2*	2.2
Low non-verbal IQ	21.0	30.3	44.4	2.1*	1.6	1.8
Low attainment	18.1	30.6	47.6	2.7*	2.0*	2.1
Unpopular	28.9	40.6	40.0	1.7*	1.7	1.0
Lacks concentration	16.1	21.2	44.4	2.3*	1.4	3.0*
Impulsive	22.0	27.3	44.4	1.8*	1.3	2.1*
Daring	20.9	51.5	55.6	4.3*	4.0*	1.2
Dishonest	19.2	40.0	42.4	2.9*	2.8*	1.1
Troublesome	14.7	28.8	64.4	4.4*	2.4*	4.5*

Notes: None = No convictions
Occ. = Occasional (1–2 convictions)
Pers. = Persistent (3+ convictions)
Del. = Delinquent (1+ convictions)
* *p* < 0.05, one-tailed

Table 1.3 Regression Analyses for Persistent Young Offenders

	OLS Regression		Logistic Regression	
	F change	p	LRCS change	p
Offender *vs*. Non-Offender				
Convicted parent	39.52	0.0001	34.49	0.0001
Daring	32.21	0.0001	38.93	0.0001
Low attainment	8.60	0.002	8.32	0.002
Poor child rearing	6.25	0.006	—	—
Poor housing	3.07	0.040	1.46	0.113
Delinquent sibling	2.93	0.044	1.29	0.128
Unpopular	1.71	0.086	4.42	0.018
Delinquent school	1.53	0.108	2.35	0.063
Large family size	—	—	3.48	0.031
Occasional *vs*. Non-Offender				
Convicted parent	32.17	0.0001	25.21	0.0001
Daring	21.85	0.0001	17.66	0.0001
Unpopular	2.67	0.052	4.85	0.014
Poor housing	1.96	0.081	3.05	0.040
Poor child rearing	1.64	0.101	1.26	0.131
Persistent *vs*. Occasional				
Low family income	5.41	0.011	7.44	0.003
Lacks concentration	3.82	0.027	—	—
Father uninvolved	3.10	0.041	—	—
Delinquent sibling	2.26	0.069	—	—
Low social class	1.40	0.121	3.17	0.038
Impulsive	—	—	1.34	0.123

Note: *p*-values one-tailed
OLS = Ordinary Least Squares
LRCS = Likelihood Ratio Chi-Squared

REFERENCES

Amdur, R. L. (1989) Testing causal models of delinquency: A methodological critique. *Criminal Justice and Behavior* 16, 35–62.

Blumstein, A., Farrington, D. P. and Moitra, S. (1985) Delinquency careers: Innocents, desisters and persisters. In M. Tonry and N. Morris (Eds.) *Crime and Justice*, vol. 6 (pp. 187–219). Chicago: University of Chicago Press.

Blumstein, A., Cohen, J. and Farrington, D. P. (1988) Criminal career research: Its value for criminology. *Criminology* 26, 1–35.

Boswell, G. (1995) *Violent Victims*. London: The Prince's Trust.

Cleary, P. D. and Angel, R. (1984) The analysis of relationships involving dichotomous dependent variables. *Journal of Health and Social Behavior* 25, 334–48.

Farrington, D. P. (1987) Early precursors of frequent offending. In J. Q. Wilson and G. C. Loury (Eds.) *From Children to Citizens*, Vol. 3: *Families, Schools and Delinquency Prevention* (pp. 27–50). New York: Springer-Verlag.

——. (1990) Implications of criminal career research for the prevention of offending. *Journal of Adolescence* 13, 93–113.

——. (1992a) Juvenile delinquency. In J. C. Coleman (Ed.) *The School Years* (2nd ed., pp. 123–63). London: Routledge.

——. (1992b) Trends in English juvenile delinquency and their explanation. *International Journal of Comparative and Applied Juvenile Justice* 16, 151–63.

——. (1993) Childhood origins of teenage antisocial behavior and adult social dysfunction. *Journal of the Royal Society of Medicine* 86, 13–17.

——. (1995) The development of offending and antisocial behavior from childhood: Key findings from the Cambridge Study in Delinquent Development. *Journal of Child Psychology and Psychiatry* 36, 929–64.

Farrington, D. P., Barnes, G. and Lambert, S. (1996) The concentration of offending in families. *Legal and Criminological Psychology* 1, 47–63.

Farrington, D. P. and Burrows, J. (1993) Did shoplifting really decrease? *British Journal of Criminology* 33, 57–69.

Farrington, D. P. and Hawkins, J. D. (1991) Predicting participation, early onset and later persistence in officially recorded offending. *Criminal Behavior and Mental Health* 1, 1–33.

Farrington, D. P., Langan, P. A. and Wikström, P.-O. H. (1994) Changes in crime and punishment in America, England and Sweden between the 1980s and 1990s. *Studies on Crime and Crime Prevention* 3, 104–31.

Farrington, D. P. and West, D. J. (1990) The Cambridge Study in Delinquent Development: A long-term follow-up of 411 London males. In H.-J. Kerner and G. Kaiser (Eds.) *Kriminalität: Persönlichkeit, Lebensgeschichte und Verhalten* (*Criminality: Personality, Behavior and Life History*) (pp. 115–38). Berlin, Germany: Springer-Verlag.

——. (1993) Criminal, penal and life histories of chronic offenders: Risk and protective factors and early identification. *Criminal Behavior and Mental Health* 3, 492–523.

Fleiss, J. L. (1981) *Statistical Methods for Rates and Proportions*. (2nd ed.) New York: Wiley.

Gottfredson, M. and Hirschi, T. (1990) *A General Theory of Crime*. Stanford, California: Stanford University Press.

Hagell, A. and Newburn, T. (1994) *Persistent Young Offenders*. London: Policy Studies Institute.

Home Office (1997) *Preventing Children Offending: A Consultation Document*. London: Home Office.

Irving, B. L. and McKenzie, I. K. (1989) *Police Interrogation*. London: Police Foundation.

LeBlanc, M. and Frechette, M. (1989) *Male Criminal Activity from Childhood through Youth.* New York: Springer-Verlag.

Moffitt, T. E. (1993) Adolescence-limited and life-course-persistent anti-social behavior: A developmental taxonomy. *Psychological Review* 100, 674–701.

Rosenthal, R. and Rubin, D. B. (1982) A simple, general-purpose display of magnitude of experimental effect. *Journal of Educational Psychology* 74, 166–69.

Schlesselman, J. J. (1982) *Case-Control Studies.* New York: Oxford University Press.

West, D. J. (1969) *Present Conduct and Future Delinquency.* London: Heinemann.

——. (1982) *Delinquency: Its Roots, Careers and Prospects.* London: Heinemann.

West, D. J. and Farrington, D. P. (1973) *Who Becomes Delinquent?* London: Heinemann.

——. (1977) *The Delinquent Way of Life.* London: Heinemann.

2 Youth Violence and the Backgrounds of Chronic Violent Offenders

Lawrence A. Greenfeld and
Maureen A. Henneberg

INTRODUCTION

Violence affects America's youth, aged 12 to 19, at higher rates than among any other age group; youth of this age account for just under 14 per cent of the population aged 12 and older, but nearly one-third of the victims of violence among residents at least 12 years old. Youth between the ages of 12 and 19 also are disproportionately responsible for violence as the perpetrators of such crimes; they account for more than a quarter of violent offenders as described by victims of violence and they account for more than a quarter of those arrested for violence by law-enforcement agencies. Our collective concern about violence and its impact on youth may be among the most challenging and difficult social problems to address. This is because we are sufficiently optimistic to believe that youth can be redirected to safer and more productive activities, and simultaneously pessimistic about knowing how to intervene effectively in their lives to reduce their vulnerability to violence, especially given the recent dramatic changes in home and family life.

MEASURING CRIME AND CRIMINAL VICTIMIZATION

There are two principal ways in which both the volume of crime and the per capita number of crimes are measured. The first involves asking the general public about their exposure to crime through the annual National Crime Victimization Survey (NCVS) sponsored by the Bureau of Justice Statistics (BJS). The second involves collecting information on crimes reported to law enforcement agencies through the Uniform Crime Reporting Program (UCR) of the Federal Bureau of Investigation (FBI). The NCVS obtains information on violent and property crimes whether or not the offense was reported to law enforcement authorities, while the UCR is limited to selected offenses known to those authorities.

The NCVS, initiated in 1973, carries out interviews about criminal victimization in six-month intervals, with household members age 12 or older, in a nationally representative sample of US households. In 1994, approximately 120000 individuals in 56000 households were interviewed twice about any crimes they may have experienced, who the perpetrator was for crimes involving personal contact between the victim-respondent and offender, and the consequences of the crime to the respondent.

The UCR, begun in 1929, collects information on reported crimes and arrests for selected types of crimes, called Part I crimes, which serve as an Index of how crime is thought to be changing based upon what is brought to the attention of law enforcement agencies. Offenses composing the Index include the following: murder and non-negligent manslaughter, forcible rape of a female victim, robbery, aggravated assault, burglary, larceny-theft, motor-vehicle theft, and arson. (Arson was added to the list of selected offenses in 1979.) In 1994, the UCR obtained such information from jurisdictions covering about 249 million residents or 96 per cent of the US population.

The NCVS permits estimation of victimization rates for subgroups of the population, an important feature for evaluating how crime affects different segments of the population. In addition, the NCVS provides details of the victim's perceptions of the characteristics of offenders. The NCVS questionnaire has undergone gradual redesign since 1989, with the goal of collecting new information on more types of crimes, particularly sexual assaults other than rape, and improving estimates of previously undisclosed crimes involving domestic violence.

VIOLENT VICTIMIZATION IS INCREASING

In 1980, the annual rate of criminal victimization, as measured by the NCVS, translated into about one violent crime for every 20 youth aged 12 to 15 years old – more than 700 000 rapes, robberies, aggravated assaults and simple assaults experienced by the nearly 15 million children of this age. By 1992, the per capita rate of violent victimization against children of this age had climbed by 50 per cent; the 14 million 12 to 15 year olds in the United States experienced nearly 1.1 million violent crimes, or one violent crime for every 13 youths of this age. In 1994, based upon the redesigned instrument which included new information on sexual assaults and more details on other violent crimes, about one in nine children aged 12 to 15 reported having been a victim of violence during the year – an estimated 1.7 million violent crimes in 1994. The violent crime experiences of 16 to 19 year olds were similar to those of 12 to 15 year olds over the period since 1980 – in 1994, about one violent crime victimization was reported among persons aged 16 to 19 for every eight persons of this age. Had the 1980 violent crime rates occurred in 1994 for those aged 12 to 19, perhaps as many as a million and a half violent crimes would not have occurred and the total volume of violent crime for all ages in the United States could have been as much as 15 per cent lower.

The most serious kind of violent criminal victimization, an attack by a gun-wielding offender, strikes those aged 16 to 19 years old at per capita rates many times that of other age groups. The gun victimization rates for those aged 16 to 19 in 1992 were more than two times the rate of those aged 25 to 34, three times the rate of those aged 35 to 49, eight times the rate of those aged 50 to 64, and finally, 17 times the rate of those aged 65 or older.

Nearly a third of robbery and assault victims aged 12 to 19 sustained a physical injury during the crime, a generally higher rate of injury than among older victims of violence. However, young people between 12 and 19 years old were the least likely of any age group to report a violent victimization to law-enforcement authorities. This was true regardless of whether the offender was a stranger or someone known to them.

The number of murder victims younger than 18 has been growing since the mid-1980s. From 1976 to 1994, the number of child murders was lowest in 1984, with 1463 children murdered, and highest in 1993, with 2841 children murdered. These increases have been concentrated in the 15- to -17 age group – from 546 in 1984 to 1480 in 1993, almost tripling in the nine-year span. Most disturbing is the 245 per cent increase of black murder victims aged 15 to 17 between the years 1984 to 1993, from 245 to 855 respectively (Figures 2.1, 2.2, and 2.3). Between 1993 and 1994 the number of child murder victims dropped by 6.4 per cent, the first decrease in a decade, but still more deaths than in any year preceding 1993.

In 1994, children under the age of 18 accounted for 11 per cent of all murder victims in the United States. Nearly half of the 2660 child victims were between ages 15 and 17 – representing the highest murder victimization rate of all age groups. In 1994, the murder rate of 13.2 murders per 100 000 resident children age 15 to 17 was 23 per cent higher than the rate for adults.

One of the most striking issues associated with violent victimization is how disproportionate it is among minority segments of the US population. African-Americans, who account for 16 per cent

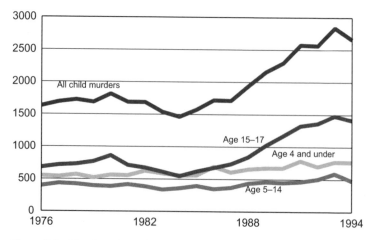

Figure 2.1 Number of murders of children, by age of victim, 1976–94

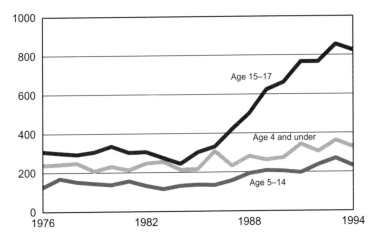

Figure 2.2 Number of murders of black children, by age of victim, 1976–94

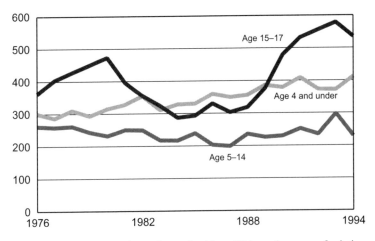

Figure 2.3 Number of murders of white children, by age of victim, 1976–94

of the population aged 12 to 15, accounted for about double that percentage of the victims of aggravated assaults. For crimes involving firearms, the disproportion is even greater. Among victims of homicides involving firearms, aged 15 to 24 years old, black males account for nearly 60 per cent of the victims while they account for about 7 per cent of all persons in that age group. Among black males and females aged 15 to 24, homicide is the leading cause of death. Among whites in the same age group, homicide is the third leading cause of death, exceeded only by accidents and suicide.

VIOLENT OFFENDING IS INCREASING

While about half the violent crimes experienced by 12 to 15 year olds involved offenders who were strangers to them, about three in five victims aged 16 to 19 reported that the offender was a stranger. About three out of four violent crime victims aged 12 to 19 described the offender as having been in the same age group. Just under 40 per cent of violent victimizations experienced by youth aged between 12 and 15 occurred at school. Youth, aged 12 to 17 years old, account for about a third of all violent crimes committed in the United States according to those victims of violence who were able to estimate the age of the offender.

Violent Offending and 15- to 17-Year-Olds

Youth aged 15 to 17 account for 13 per cent of all arrests nationwide for Part I violent crimes as defined by the Federal Bureau of Investigation (murder and non-negligent manslaughter, forcible rape, robbery, and aggravated assault) and seven out of ten violent juvenile arrestees are in this age group. Thus, it is important to understand how this group is changing in both size and extent of involvement in violent crime.

Figure 2.4 shows the cumulative number of arrests for violence between the ages of 15 and 17 years by year of birth. As can be seen, each birth cohort in the latter half of the 1960s (who would have turned 17 during the mid-1980s) accumulated about 60 000 arrests for violence between 15 and 17 years old. Cohorts born in each year of the 1970s showed a consistent increase in the volume of arrests for violence acquired by age 17. The 1978 cohort was the first and only to surpass 100 000 violent arrests between the ages of 15 and 17 (those born in 1978 reached age 17 in 1995). Figure 2.5 translates these cumulative numbers of arrests for violence into per capita rates which take into account the size of the birth cohort. Each birth cohort, beginning in 1971, evidences a

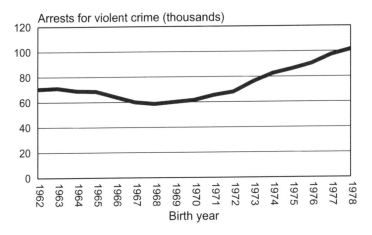

Figure 2.4   Estimate of the cumulative number of arrests for violent crimes between ages 15 and 17, by birth year

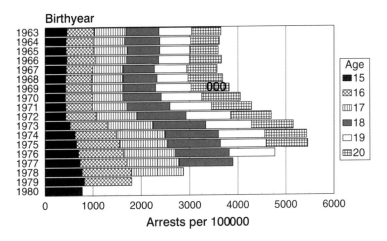

Figure 2.5   Number of arrests for violent crime per 100 000 by birth year, ages 15 to 20

higher arrest rate for violence than the preceding one at each age. By age 17 the 1977 birth cohort had acquired about 1000 more arrests for violence per 100 000 members than the 1963 cohort. Arrestees born in 1979, who turned 15 in 1994, were more violent than any of their predecessors, while those born in 1980 evidenced the first reduction in the per capita number of violent arrests at age 15.

The finding that the more recent birth cohorts have been more criminally active than prior cohorts can also be illustrated with data drawn from a national survey of state prison inmates conducted in 1991 by the Bureau of Justice Statistics. As can be seen in Figure 2.6, the youngest inmates serving time in state prisons in 1991 were the most likely to have had a juvenile arrest history, with a sharp increase in such a history among those born in the early 1970s. About five out of ten inmates serving time in 1991 reported having been arrested as a child. Most inmates with prior arrests report that their first arrest occurred when they were 15 to 17 years old (Figure 2.7).

The growth in arrest rates for violence among 15-, 16-, and 17-year-olds has been dramatic, but at the same time the number of such persons in the general population has been declining.

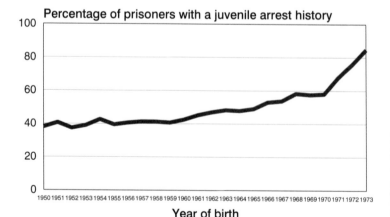

Figure 2.6 Prevalence of juvenile arrest history among State prison immates in 1991, by year of birth

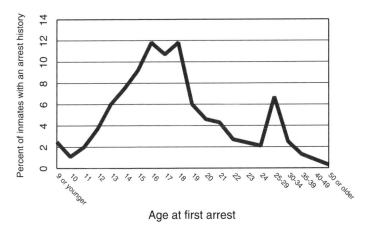

Figure 2.7   Age at first arrest for prisoners with a prior arrest history, 1991

In 1976, almost 13 million persons were in this age group compared to just over 10 million in 1991. In 1994, there were 10.7 million persons between the ages of 15 and 17. The population will peak again in 2005 at 11.7 million persons aged 15 to 17. However, if the increases in the rate of arrest for violence observed over the last two decades continue, averaging 3 to 4 per cent annually, a large increase in the number of juvenile arrests for violence will be recorded a decade from now, perhaps reaching as high as twice the number in 1994.

Aside from the growth in arrests and arrest rates for violent offenses among persons aged 15 to 17, there has also been a sharp increase in arrests for weapons offenses among this age group. A recent survey of 758 male students in ten inner-city high schools found that 22 per cent of the students possessed firearms. This striking finding illustrates what has been seen in the numbers of arrests for weapons violations among youth – compared to 1980, the number of arrests for weapons offenses in 1994 reflected an increase of 241 per cent among children aged 14 and younger and 149 per cent among all those less than 18 years old. By contrast, there was a 39 per cent increase in the number of arrests for weapons violations among those 18 or older over the same period. Compared to 1980, black youth, aged 17 and younger, have experienced nearly twice the rate of increase of whites of the same age for weapons violations – just over one-third of the juveniles arrested for weapons offenses in 1994 were black.

The Increasing Seriousness of Juvenile Offending

Aside from the problem of increased rates of violent offending among youth, there is also concern about the quality of the violent acts associated with youth. In 1980, juveniles 17 years old and younger accounted for just over 8 per cent of the murders in which the identity of the murderer was known to law enforcement authorities; by 1994 that figure had doubled to 16 per cent. During the same period the share of firearm murders associated with juvenile offenders grew from 7.5 per cent of all firearm murder victims to more than 18 per cent, from 882 in 1980 to 2457 in 1994, which is about ten times the rate of change in all murders with known perpetrators using firearms.

In 1976 an estimated 25 per cent of child murders where the offender was known were committed by persons 17 and younger. In 1994, this number was nearly 30 per cent. Over the period since 1976, for those child murders where the offender was known, children murdering children grew at twice the rate as adults murdering children (73 versus 36 per cent) (Figure 2.8). In 1994, of those child murders where the offender was known to be a child, more than six out of ten were committed by 16 and 17 year olds.

In 1994, based upon responses to the National Crime Victimization Survey, victims of robbery and aggravated assault reported that more than four out of ten perpetrators of these crimes were perceived to be between the ages of 12 and 20 years old. In 1987, less than 30 per cent of the victims of these crimes identified the offenders as between the ages of 12 and 20 years old. Robbery and aggravated assault are serious violent crimes for which victims are, to a large and stable extent over time, capable of describing the perpetrator. Furthermore, they are offenses largely unaffected by the redesigned NCVS which was first fielded in 1992.

In 1987, victims attributed nearly 700 000 robberies and aggravated assaults to offenders under the age of 21. In 1994, victims estimated that nearly 1.4 million robberies and aggravated assaults

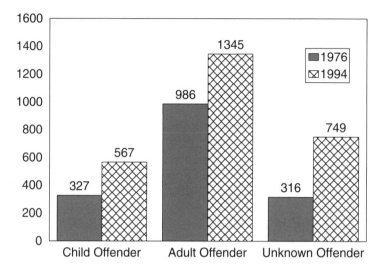

Figure 2.8 Number of murders of victims under age 18, by age of offender 1976 & 1994

were carried out by youth of this age. For both robbery and aggravated assault, the numbers of each crime in which youth had been the offenders were reported by victims to have doubled over the period.

A significant aspect of the change in the volume of serious youth crime has been the growth in the percentage of these crimes attributable to *groups* of youths, all aged 12 to 20 years old. In 1987, about one in ten robberies and aggravated assaults was perpetrated by two or more youth according to victims; in 1994, nearly one in 5 robberies and aggravated assaults was committed by groups of youth aged 12 to 20.

Using the number of robberies and aggravated assaults committed by youth aged 12 to 20 as the numerator, with the number of resident youth of that age in the denominator, it is possible to calculate the 'rate of victimizing' or the number of such crimes relative to the size of the age cohort. In 1987, there was about one robbery or aggravated assault committed by a youth aged 12 to 20 for every 47 youth of that age. In 1994, the 'victimizing rate' had doubled to about one robbery or aggravated assault committed by a youth for every 23 youth in the resident population. The increased 'rate of victimizing' has led to increased fear of violence perpetrated by youth among young people. In 1995 the National Crime Victimization Survey asked students age 12 to 19, representing an estimated 24 million students, about their perceptions regarding various crime issues, such as how prevalent street gangs were in school and how fearful students were of being attacked at school. One out of four students reported gang presence at their school. Among all students, those who reported the presence of gangs were more likely than students from schools without gangs to be victims of some type of crime. An earlier study found that students at schools with gangs were about twice as likely as students from schools without gangs to be afraid of attack, both at school and traveling to and from school.

EXAMINING THE CHRONIC VIOLENT OFFENDER

Every five years, the Bureau of Justice Statistics conducts a survey among a nationally representative sample of state prisoners to learn more about their family and social backgrounds, their criminal careers and their use and abuse of alcohol and drugs. Surveys have been conducted in 1974, 1979, 1986, 1991, and most recently in 1997 (to be released shortly). The 1991 survey conducted personal interviews among 14 000 prisoners held in nearly 300 prisons to obtain detailed information about their lives not generally available in official records. Among the most interesting are the descriptions of home-life and upbringing.

The vast majority of state prisoners in the United States have a history of arrests preceding the arrest which brought them to prison – for about half of these, the first arrest for a criminal charge occurred before they reached the age of 18 (Figure 2.9). An estimated two-thirds of prisoners with criminal careers of at least 16 years' duration reported that their first arrest occurred when they were younger than 18 years old. About 8 per cent of state prisoners reported that their first arrest as a juvenile was for a violent crime, and the youngest inmates were more likely to report that their first arrest was for a violent crime (Figure 2.10).

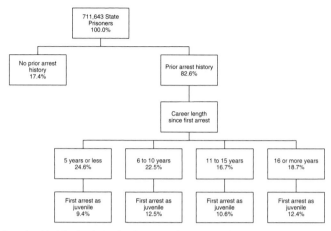

Career length is defined as the time from first arrest to the arrest for which an inmate was serving time in 1991.

Figure 2.9   Arrest history and length of criminal career of State prison inmates, 1991

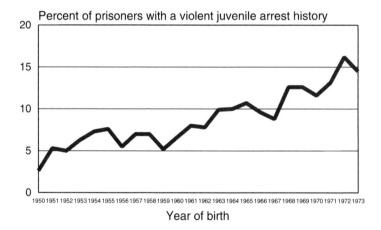

Figure 2.10   Prevalence of violent juvenile arrest history among State prison inmates in 1991, by year of birth

An estimated 38 per cent of those serving time in state prisons have a history of convictions by the juvenile justice system resulting in sentences to confinement or probation (Figure 2.11). There was no difference in the juvenile conviction background of

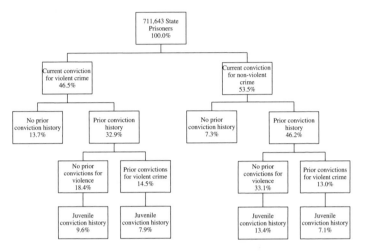

Conviction history is based on those offenses which resulted in a sentence to probation or confinement.

Figure 2.11   Violence and conviction history of State prison inmates, 1991

violent and non-violent offenders serving time in state prisons in 1991 – an estimated 38 per cent of inmates serving time after conviction for a violent offense had a history of juvenile convictions, and 38 per cent of those imprisoned for non-violent offenses had a history of prior juvenile convictions.

Substantial variation in juvenile conviction history was found, however, when the inmates were examined by offense (Table 2.1). While more than half of those in prison for burglary and motor vehicle theft reported a juvenile conviction history, only about a quarter of those convicted of negligent manslaughter, sexual assaults other than rape, and possession of drugs reported a background of juvenile convictions. One in three prisoners convicted of burglary or motor vehicle theft reported multiple juvenile convictions. An estimated 7 per cent of all state prisoners had at least three juvenile convictions and at least three prior adult convictions before the current conviction for which they were serving time in 1991 (Table 2.2).

The 1991 BJS Survey of State Prison Inmates reveals that about 11 per cent of prisoners describe a career of chronic violence with convictions for violent crimes extending across their juvenile years into adulthood. Criminal histories gathered from the prisoners indicate that, for about half of all prisoners, their first violent conviction came as an adult, another 2 per cent reported that their only history of violence was as a juvenile, and just under 39 per cent report no history of violence at all prior to the crime for which they were serving time.

About two-thirds of the chronically violent, with adult and juvenile histories of violence, reported that they had primarily grown up in something other than a two-parent household – about half the chronic offenders were raised by a mother alone. By contrast, nearly half of the prisoners who were violent only as adults or who had never been violent said they had grown up in a two-parent household – about a third had lived in a mother-only household. Chronic violent offenders were about twice as likely as other offenders to have spent some part of their early years in a foster home or an institution. While an estimated 37 per cent of the chronically violent had spent some time in a foster home or other institution, only about 15 per cent of the other offenders had experienced such living arrangements during their childhood years. Chronic violent offenders were also more likely than other offenders to report that their parents or foster parents had abused drugs or alcohol. They were twice as likely as other offenders to report that both drugs and alcohol had been abused by parents in the home.

More than half of the chronically violent offenders reported that an immediate family member had served time. About a third of the other imprisoned offenders reported prior incarceration among an immediate family member. Chronic violent offenders were about twice as likely to have had a mother, father, or sister who had served time and about a third more likely to have had a brother who served time. There were no apparent differences between the chronically violent and other prisoners in experiences with physical or sexual abuse.

In general, the survey data indicate that the chronically violent are distinguishable from other offenders in terms of the characteristics of their upbringing and their home and family lives. In particular, the majority of the chronically violent come from disordered and chaotic family backgrounds.

IMPLICATIONS FOR PUBLIC POLICY

National arrest statistics clearly show that today's youth are more involved in violent crime than equivalent age groups in years past. Similarly, the youngest prisoners report more substantial involvement in the juvenile justice system and longer records of violent juvenile conduct than older inmates. In terms of public policy, a significant finding is the problematic family backgrounds which the chronically violent are most likely to have experienced, with only a small minority actually having experienced the presence of two parents during their childhood. This is significant because of the changes which have been taking place in the American family. A decade ago, 18 per cent of births in the United States were to unmarried women, while today that figure is 30 per cent. In 1970, 6 per cent of white births were to an unmarried woman, while by 1994 that figure had risen to 25 per cent. In 1970, 38 per cent of births among African-American women were out of wedlock, while in 1994 a staggering 70 per cent of black births were to unmarried women. The young people who are experiencing the rapid increases in violence observed since 1987, as both victims and offenders, were all born during the period when this rapid change in family structure occurred.

In addition, increasing criminal experience among the most recent cohorts maturing through the latter teenage years has implications for the prevalence of imprisonment among future populations. In 1991, an estimated 5.4 per cent of all black males in their twenties were serving time in state prisons on any given day compared to about 0.8 per cent of white males in their twenties. By comparison, in 1974 the daily incarceration rates for males in their twenties was 2.6 per cent of blacks and 0.3 per cent of whites. Such daily rates translate into substantially larger lifetime prevalences – in 1974, the lifetime probability of imprisonment was 2 per cent for white males and 14 per cent for black males. Estimates for 1991 indicate that about one in four black males and about one in 25 white males could be expected to serve at least one term of imprisonment in their lifetime. These are substantially higher lifetime probabilities of imprisonment than those found in earlier life-table projections based upon the self-reports of inmates.

In addition to their confinement histories, prisoners in 1991 also self-reported more extensive backgrounds of probation prior to imprisonment – inmates in 1991 were twice as likely as inmates a decade ago to have had three or more prior probation sentences. Thus, inmates today not only have more extensive juvenile records than in the past, but have also received more bites of the probation apple, prior to their current imprisonment, than earlier samples of prisoners.

An obvious goal of learning about the juvenile criminal careers of adult offenders would be the prediction and treatment of those developmental factors most associated with future criminality among youth. Table 2.3 shows that among those serving time in state prisons in 1991, the largest proportion of convicted violent offenders had their first arrest as a juvenile for a non-violent crime – 17 per cent of all prisoners were first arrested as juveniles for a non-violent crime and were incarcerated at the time of the survey for a violent offense as adults. What is more important is that those first arrested for violence as adults or juveniles had nearly identical current offense distributions; that is, while about 8 per cent of prisoners were first arrested as juveniles for violence and 7 per cent of prisoners were first arrested for violence as adults, the percentage serving time in 1991 for violent, property, drug, and public-order offenses was identical within the two groups. In other words, the current offense of those in state prison appears to have little to do with whether their first arrest for violence occurred as juveniles or adults.

One cautionary note about these data must be kept in mind, however. Knowledge based upon inmate surveys lacks the necessary comparative information about those with first arrests as juveniles who then desisted from crime. Efforts to predict adult offending based upon self-report surveys from known adult offenders is of limited value for reshaping responses to juvenile criminality. Complementary research on those who drop out of crime is as important to learning about criminal careers and testing and evaluating public policies as studying only those who continue offending.

None the less, the value of inmate survey data is that they help us to draw reasonable inferences about those characteristics found with higher prevalence among prisoners than is the case among similar age, race, and sex cohorts in the general population, and particularly those with chronic criminal careers extending across childhood and adulthood. These identifiable differences between offenders and the general population represent important data concerns and may provide more fertile ground for shaping adult programs and sanctions. While we know, for example, that the average chronically violent offender may come from a very different home and family background than the general population, we still do not know very much about exactly how or why family background influences those who discontinue a criminal lifestyle while still in their juvenile years.

The increased violence among teenage cohorts now entering adulthood, the dramatic change in family background among today's teenagers and their increasing involvement with the juvenile and criminal justice systems, particularly imprisonment, poses important public policy questions for the future as the size of youth cohorts grows. The reason for our concern with public policy is the recognition that the increasing vulnerability to violence among youth and their increased number represents a challenge for us today as well as an ominous statement about their future. These policy questions, at the most basic level, relate to the realities of what families and governments at all levels are capable of doing (and not doing) during a child's development.

For the last couple of years the US Department of Justice has announced good news about youth crime. National data show that the per capita violent crime arrest rate among juveniles declined by almost 3 per cent in 1995, reaching approximately the rate recorded two years earlier. During 1996 an even larger decrease in the rate of arrest for violence occurred among juveniles, bringing the total decline since 1994 to nearly 13 per cent. The last annual decrease occurred in 1987. Over the last decade, violent crime arrest rates for juveniles peaked in 1994, after rising by nearly two-thirds since 1987 (from 311 arrests for violence per 100 000 youth aged 10 to 17 in 1987 to a rate of 513 per 100 000 in 1994). Between 1994 and 1996, the rate declined nearly 13 per cent to

448 per 100 000. Arrest data for 1995 also show that the violent crime arrest rate for 15-year-olds dropped for the first time since 1985, equaling the per capita rate for 15-year-olds in 1993. While recent changes may be a slight improvement, current rates of arrest for violent crime by juveniles are well above the rates in the 290s per 100 000 recorded in 1983 and 1984. Furthermore, the arrest rate among juveniles for murder in 1995 was about double the murder arrest rate recorded 10 years earlier (11.2 as compared with 5.7) and was 15 per cent higher than the murder arrest rate among adults (11.2 as compared with 9.7).

Trends in arrest rates for violence among youth by year of birth show that there has been continued improvement among the younger cohorts. Those born in 1979, for example, experienced an arrest rate for violence of 822 arrests per 100 000 when they reached age 15 in 1994. By contrast, those born in 1981 had an arrest rate which was 15 per cent lower when they reached age 15 in 1996 (696 arrests per 100 000). Though a substantial improvement, the 15-year-olds in 1996 still had a per capita arrest rate for violence which was 61 per cent higher than that of 15-year-olds in 1986 (those born in 1971 had an arrest rate in 1986 of 432 per 100 000).

Monitoring these trends in a systematic way will be an essential element in gauging whether the policy choices adopted based upon predicted causal links to adult criminality avert what seems to be a slide into more criminally active lifestyles among children. Whether growth in violent criminal activity among cohorts moving through the teenage years continues and whether, as the data suggest, an ever-growing fraction of prisoners have such histories of juvenile criminality will depend upon many factors. One which is most intriguing is the apparent contemporaneous changes in family structure. New initiatives, such as prosecuting predatory juvenile offenders as adults, changing the status of the juvenile criminal history records, experimenting with school uniforms, or changing the rules for welfare assistance, will all require substantial evaluation aimed at determining, in the near and the long term, the impact on the rates of juvenile criminality and the likelihood of a subsequent adult criminal career. The most

difficult challenge amidst all these policy changes is the need
to learn which public policies we initiate actually encourage,
discourage, or have no effect on dropping out of crime during the
juvenile years and desisting from crime during the adult years.

Table 2.1   Juvenile conviction histories of State prison inmates,
by current conviction offense, 1991

Current offense	Number of prisoners	Number of juvenile convictions (%)			
		None	One	Two	Three or more
Violent	327,958	61.7	18.2	9.5	10.7
Murder	74,693	62.7	17.3	10.3	9.6
Negligent manslaughter	12,786	75.4	16.2	4.3	4.1
Kidnapping	8,369	55.5	17.8	10.6	16.1
Rape	24,833	66.4	17.5	6.6	9.5
Other sexual assault	41,649	77.3	13.2	4.1	5.3
Robbery	104,136	52.5	21.5	12.1	13.9
Assault	57,558	61.3	17.8	9.8	11.1
Other violent	3,934	68.6	13.5	7.1	10.9
Property	174,534	53.3	19.8	10.8	16.2
Burglary	87,515	48.4	21.5	12.2	18.0
Larceny	34,342	57.0	19.7	10.8	12.6
Motor vehicle theft	15,276	47.4	17.6	12.9	22.2
Arson	4,753	59.7	20.3	6.0	14.0
Fraud	19,769	66.7	15.5	6.4	11.3
Stolen property	9,800	59.1	17.5	5.9	17.4
Other property	3,079	63.4	15.9	11.1	9.6
Drugs	150,304	70.1	15.8	6.9	7.3
Possession	53,264	73.5	13.1	6.7	6.6
Trafficking	93,839	68.3	17.3	6.8	7.5
Other drugs	3,202	67.4	13.9	9.2	9.5
Public order	48,452	62.1	17.3	7.6	12.9
Weapons	12,723	58.7	22.8	8.5	10.1
Other public order	35,729	63.4	15.4	7.3	14.0
Other	10,395	75.4	12.5	5.5	6.5
Total	711,643	61.7	17.9	9.0	11.4

Table 2.2 Juvenile and adult conviction histories of
State prison inmates, 1991

Number of adult convictions	Number of prior juvenile convictions				
	None	One	Two	Three or more	Total
None	20.4	4.9	1.7	1.4	28.5
One	14.5	4.4	1.7	1.3	21.9
Two	10.1	3.4	1.9	1.9	17.3
Three or more	16.6	5.2	3.8	6.7	32.3
Total	61.7	17.9	9.0	11.4	100.0

Note: Convictions are those dispositions in which a sentence to confinement or probation was imposed.

Table 2.3 Age at first arrest, type of first arrest offense, and current conviction offense, State prisoners, 1991

	First arrest age and offense					
Current offense	Juvenile arrest crime was		Adult arrest crime was		No prior arrests	Total
	Violent	Non-violent	Violent	Non-violent		
Violent	4.3	17.0	4.2	11.1	10.4	46.8
Property	1.7	11.6	1.2	7.9	2.3	24.8
Drugs	1.5	6.3	1.4	8.5	3.8	21.5
Public order	0.5	2.5	0.5	2.7	0.6	6.9
Total	8.0	37.4	7.3	30.3	17.1	100.0

Note: Table based upon 704 181 State prison inmates for whom age at first arrest and type of arrest offense were known.

Part II
Problems in British and American Juvenile Justice

3 The New Political Consensus on Youth Justice in Britain

Andrew Rutherford

During the 1980s concerted efforts were made at the level of both policy and practice to fashion an approach to youth justice which was rational, reflective, and humane. By the end of the decade considerable progress in this direction had been achieved. Paradoxically, all of this took place during the 'Thatcher years', but in the realm of criminal justice, for the most part, 'one-nation' Toryism held sway (Windlesham, 1993; Rutherford, 1996). The task for the 1990s seemed largely to be one of consolidation (Rutherford, 1992; Gelsthorpe and Morris, 1994). However, within the space of no more than two years most of the gains had been undone and the tone and direction of policy had been radically transformed. This remarkable *volte face* of youth justice in England and Wales underlines the inherent vulnerability of socio-liberal patterns to criminal policy.

The defining feature of youth justice in Britain during the 1980s was that of de-escalation at virtually every stage of process. In the first instance, the police became increasingly proactive in using the least formal means of intervention. Informal warnings were preferred to formal cautions, and wherever possible court proceedings were avoided by the use of formal cautions. For the police to issue a formal caution, the individual had to admit guilt to a senior police officer (or, in the case of a juvenile, in the presence of a parent or other responsible adult). Furthermore, a record of the formal caution is available in the event of a subsequent court appearance at the sentencing stage of the proceedings.

Little is known about the number of informal warnings issued, but the Home Office statistics reveal an unequivocal endorsement of the principle of minimum intervention. In 1980, 90 200 juveniles (children aged 10 to 17) were found guilty by the courts. In 1990 the total was 24 700, representing a 73 per cent decline in court caseloads over the decade.[1] While the actual number of formal cautions remained relatively stable, as a proportion of 'known offenders' (i.e. formal cautions plus guilt findings) there was an increase from 49 to 78 per cent. While the proportionate use of formal cautioning had substantially increased during the previous decade, growth occurred at a rather slower pace. In this regard the police can be considered as the harbingers of the youth justice reforms which flowered in the 1980s. However, the involvement of some police officers in the subsequent reaction points to conflicts within the police organization which await full exploration.

It is also evident from the official figures, and this was to become a matter of considerable controversy, that over this period the total number of 'known offenders' declined by 37 per cent. The direction of this discretionary practice by most police forces was encouraged through the Home Office in advice to chief constables and other senior practitioners. For example, a 1985 Home Office circular stated that, for juveniles, 'there may be positive advantages for society, as well as for the individual, in using prosecution as a last resort'. More recently, with reference to juveniles and young adults (17- to 20-year-olds), the Home Office urged in 1990 that prosecution 'should only be used as a last resort'.

With the courts receiving a much reduced but relatively more serious group of young offenders, it might have been expected that more severe sentences would be imposed. The reverse, however, occurred, and the de-escalatory trend is as apparent within the court setting as at earlier stages of the process. Over the decade there was an 81 per cent decline in the use of custodial sentences for boys aged 14 to 16 (this compares with a 112 per cent increase in the use of custody for this group over the 1970s). It is also striking that the use of discharges for juvenile offenders also substantially increased during the 1980s.

To a considerable extent these de-escalatory statistical trends reflected an emerging confluence of practitioners and policymakers, especially during the latter part of the period. A host of local projects sprang up across the country, many of which were the result of successful collaboration across organizational boundaries. The intent was to develop effective community-based activities for young people, but also to change the direction of decision-making at all stages of the process. There was a powerful sense among practitioners that change lay in their hands, that they were able to set the pace and that policy would follow in the wake of well-tried developments on the ground (see Rutherford, 1992, 1993, for further discussion). In retrospect it can be seen to have been a two-way relationship reflecting important elements of a new policy framework in the opening years and a receptiveness on the part of policy-makers to learn from the lessons emerging from local good practice (Rutherford, 1992, 1993; Wade, 1996). A significant element of this new framework was the initiative by the Department of Health and Social Security of a £15 million grant to encourage local 'intermediate treatment' projects, which provided an impetus and encouragement to local authorities and the voluntary sector to set up schemes that might serve as alternatives to custody. A Local Authority circular in 1983 announced that some ninety local projects were funded under this scheme.

Around the same time, a new sentencing framework for young offenders was introduced under the Criminal Justice Act of 1982. As a result of persistent and skilful backbench parliamentary maneuvering in both the House of Commons and House of Lords, the original bill had been enhanced (despite the government's opposition) through the introduction of minimum statutory criteria which had to be satisfied (in most instances) before a custodial sentence could be imposed. By the end of the decade it was clear that these provisions were biting on day-to-day practice in the courts. In 1986 a senior Home Office official, David Faulkner, told a meeting of magistrates that the principle he wished to suggest for juvenile justice was that of 'minimum intervention'. He went on to say that although it was not expressed this way during the passage of the 1982 Act, 'it is a theme which runs through all its juvenile justice provisions' (Rutherford, 1996, p. 107).

From 1986–7 onwards, the notion of minimum intervention for juvenile offenders was established at the levels of policy and practice. The policy challenge for the future was the extent to which this approach might be extended to young adult and, indeed, adult offenders. The government's Green Paper of June 1988 clearly stated that imprisonment limited the offender's personal responsibility for making everyday decisions, thereby diminishing the individual's sense of responsibility and self-reliance. As David Faulkner pointed out, 'the proposals in the Green Paper start from the successful experience with juveniles, and the lack of evidence that an increase in the use of community sentences would lead to an increase in crime, or put the public at risk' (Rutherford, 1996, p. 103). Speaking of 'the teenage thief' at the Conservative Party Conference in October 1988, the then Home Secretary, Douglas Hurd, remarked that rather than 'idling in a prison cell...we can put him to something useful', such as employment, which also allows the offender to compensate his victim. The courts would therefore be provided with 'a wider and tougher range of these community-based punishments'.

The main thrust of these ideas were carried forward in the Home Office White Paper of February 1990, and in the subsequent criminal justice legislation. But by this time Douglas Hurd had moved to the Foreign Office, and David Faulkner had been transferred to other responsibilities within the Home Office. The Criminal Justice Act 1991 replaced the juvenile court with the 'youth court', and brought 17-year-olds within its jurisdiction (see generally Ashworth and Gibson, 1994). The Act also barred 14-year-old boys from custodial sentences, placing them in the position that girls of that age had held for some years (Rutherford, 1992). Important as these measures were, the main thrust of the legislation had the broader purpose of fashioning a sentencing framework for the courts, regardless of the offender's age. However, despite the efforts of ministers and officials to gain the support of senior judges, from the start the Criminal Justice Act 1991 was viewed with deep suspicion by the judiciary. Indeed, the Act became the focal point of the rejection of much of what had been achieved during the previous decade.[2]

The reaction, when it came in 1992–3, was remarkable in its rapidity and ferocity. By the mid-1990s most traces of the socio-liberal model at the level of policy had been erased. All that remained in the area of youth justice were valiant localized efforts by youth justice practitioners, against mounting odds, to keep procedures and structures in place. The trends after 1992 were consistently escalatory in direction.[3] The reaction was to criminal policy in general, but it was particularly evident with respect to youth justice. It was in this area, where the most progress in the socio-liberal direction had been made, that opposition was most evident. Youth justice was therefore at the fore, with respect to both the advances gained in the 1980s and to the retreats of the 1990s. The following account of this reversal, which David Faulkner has described as 'the most sudden and the most radical which has ever taken place in this area of public policy', highlights in particular the transformation of discourse adopted by the two main political parties (Faulkner, 1993).

By the mid-1990s both the Conservative and Labour Parties had moved onto new ground with respect to youth justice and criminal policy generally. In large part the perceived vulnerability of the position adopted by the government in the latter 1980s had become a common target of the two main political parties. These new postures began to take shape as the House of Commons Select Committee on Home Affairs commenced an enquiry into young offenders in the autumn of 1992. Inevitably, the Select Committee was perplexed as to whether or not youth crime had increased during the 1980s. The air of uncertainty which characterized the government's position was all too evident. While acknowledging that there could be no precision as to the actual level of crime committed by juveniles, the Home Office's evidence pointed out that the number of 10- to 17-year-olds who were known offenders had fallen both in absolute terms and as a rate per age group in the population. But the overall level of offenses recorded by the police had risen in recent years, and the extensive media coverage suggested heightened public concern. The Select Committee's synthesis of the conflicting evidence it received foreshadowed the emerging role of the persistent offender within the realm of public policy. The Select Committee concluded:

> If there is a small but growing number of juvenile offenders responsible for many offenses (some of which they may be convicted or cautioned for and some of which may go undetected) it is possible to reconcile the indisputable fact that the number

(and rate, to a lesser extent) of known juvenile offenders has fallen over time with the more speculative assertion that the number of offenses committed by juveniles has risen. (Home Affairs Select Committee, 1993, p. xii)

In its evidence to the Select Committee, the Association of Chief Police Officers estimated that there had been a 54 per cent increase in juvenile crime over the last 10 years. Paul Cavadino commented that this

> [S]eems to have been a completely bogus figure, because they started from official recorded crime statistics, showing a drop in the number of juvenile crimes recorded, [and] they then said, 'However, there has been a 25 per cent drop in the juvenile population and if the juvenile population had stayed as it was ten years ago we would have had *pro rata* another 95 900 crimes', so a substantial step in their working was to invent a non-existent 75 900 crimes that would have been committed by the non-existent juveniles. (Home Affairs Select Committee, 1993, p. 288)

Understandably, by the time the Select Committee's report was published in July 1993 the government had abandoned all claims that crime by young people was declining. But there were indications of the political turn on youth justice before the Select Committee decided upon its enquiry. For example, during Kenneth Baker's period as Home Secretary, from November 1990 to April 1992, the focus was very much upon car theft and offending on bail. Concerted campaigns by some police officers, effectively using links with the media, played a crucial role. One rapid response at this time was the Aggravated Vehicle-Taking Act 1991, which was the first of two series of hastily conceived and constructed statutes which weakened the spirit and principles of the Criminal Justice Act of 1991. (The direct weakening of the 1991 Act's sentencing provisions came later with the Criminal Justice Act 1993.) In addition, the phrase 'bail bandit' (a person who offends while on bail) was invented by a police spokesperson, popularized by the Home Secretary, and found a regular place in tabloid newspaper headlines. Mr Baker also expressed anxiety about persistent young offenders and the need to increase the amount of secure accommodation.

There were also early indications that the position of the Labour Party was being reassessed. In January 1992 the Labour Party Deputy Leader and spokesperson on home affairs, Roy Hattersley, taunted the government over an 18 per cent rise in recorded crime over the previous two years. Simon Heffer commented in a conservative weekly, 'Most of the policies that failed the Tory party on law and order in its first ten years in office (similar to those that failed the Wilson, Heath and Callaghan governments before) have been abandoned, stealthily and subtly, but abandoned nonetheless' (Heffer, 1992). Feeling cheered by all this, Heffer concluded that:

> As long as the Government is not too shy to proclaim its change of heart, it can match the new moral Labour Party on the law and order question, despite its abysmal record. But the change must be signalled uncompromisingly, no matter how many liberals and anti-authoritarians it offends. Mr Kenneth Clarke, the Education Secretary, has done just that with his policy, and with great success. (Heffer, 1992)

After the return of the Conservatives to office two months later, Mr Clarke was transferred to the Home Office, with Heffer now commenting that he was cynical about 'community' treatments. Regarding approved schools, which were descendants of nineteenth-century reformatories and industrial schools and existed in Britain until the early 1970s, Heffer wrote, 'Approved schools might just about keep everybody happy. All that stands in the way of their return is not political feasibility, but political will' (1993a). As to Mr Hurd's orientation towards community penalties: 'The folly of this keep-them-out-at-all-costs policy was soon recognized, but is only now being reversed ... Even they (the Home Office civil servants) could not ignore the crime figures. ... These days Mr Hurd is the nearest thing to a saint we have in Government. ... It is at this door, however, that many current crime and policing problems must be laid' (Heffer, 1993b, p. 6).

At the same time as Mr Clarke became Home Secretary, his new opposite number on the Labour Party's front benches was

Tony Blair, currently Prime Minister. In one of their first public confrontations, on a radio news program, Blair spoke of being 'tough on crime and tough on the causes of crime'. It was this phrase, more than any other, which signalled the turn in Labour's thinking on the issue. The Labour Party's evidence to the Select Committee stated that it was 'difficult to believe Home Office claims that offending by young people has actually gone down across the country' (Home Affairs Select Committee, 1993, p. 392). 'The instinctive reaction of most people faced with an escalation of serious crimes by young people is to say "if they won't stop, they should be locked away". We agree – but we think it fair to ask whether society has tried to stop such youngsters from offending' (p. 393). The Labour Party also called for 'practical and tough-minded intervention at an early age' (p. 398). In early February 1993 the abduction (recorded by a security video camera and to become haunting footage for television) and subsequent murder of 2-year-old James Bulger by two 10-year-old boys galvanized public anxieties in an extraordinary way. In this new situation Mr Clarke ditched work on a White Paper and proceeded directly with proposals for secure training centres. This was first announced in an article prepared for a national newspaper, in which the Home Secretary said that his main priority since taking up office had been to ensure right response to young offenders. The focus needed to be on the relatively small group of youngsters who committed a disproportionate number of crimes. At this time, though, the elusive nature of the persistent offender was reinforced by research commissioned by the Home Office (see Newburn and Hagell, 1994). 'There is an absence of secure facilities ... and a new sentence is required ... providing education, training and support, giving not just the discipline but the affection which they clearly need but which has never been effectively provided in their own home' (Clarke, 1993; he also promised to reduce repeat cautioning and deal with persons who commit offenses on bail). A few days later, Clarke told the House of Commons on 2 March 1993 that supervision orders were 'necessary and sensible for the great majority of juvenile offenders, but I have decided that they are insufficient to deal effectively with that comparatively small group of persistent offenders whose repeated offenses makes them a menace to the community. For such persons a secure training order would be added to the sentencing powers of the courts.' In a subsequent interview, Mr Clarke, after commenting that he did not 'come from the Whiggish end of the Conservative Party', remarked: 'There must be somewhere in the Treasury somebody who thinks the problem of juvenile offenders is now entirely cured because there are none of them locked up at public expense. The trouble is, the problem has transferred itself to the housing estates of England '(Heffer, 1993a).

The proposal for secure training centers for 12- to 14-year-olds represented a direct and total rejection of the Hurd era. By striking at young offenders and focusing as much on previous record as immediate offense, secure training centres marked the wholesale rejection of the underlying principles embedded in the Criminal Justice Act of 1991. This was a theme enthusiastically pursued by Michael Howard, who succeeded Mr Clarke at the Home Office during the summer of 1993. Addressing the Conservative Party Conference in October, in the course of his 'prison works' speech, Mr Howard declared: 'We must get on, pass the legislation, build these centres and take these young thugs off the streets.' Among a total of 27 measures announced by Mr Howard was the tightening up of cautioning practice by the police. A new Home Office circular, issued a few months later in 1994, advised that only in exceptional circumstances should a second caution be given. Although these instructions on cautioning took immediate effect, proceeding with secure training centres had to await passage of the Criminal Justice and Public Order Act 1994 and long-drawn-out planning and contracting-out procedures. When the bill was before Parliament the position of the Labour Party was to abstain. None the less, aspects of the proposals on secure training centres did encounter sustained opposition in the House of Lords from a group of peers from all parties (as well as independents), under the unofficial leadership of the Conservative peer, the late Lucy Faithful. Although secure training orders survived, it remained uncertain whether even one of the five proposed centres would be opened before the general election, which had to take place by May 1997. Labour's position was that while any contracts with private sector providers would be honored, 'we would review the inherited position on the government's "heard but not seen" secure residential training centres and use the resources to best advantage under our new strategy' (Labour Party, 1996, p. 15).

The 1990s may have opened with the appearances of 'a return to the consensus on crime that marked the post-war era' (Gelsthorpe and Morris, 1994, p. 983) but this was swiftly overtaken by a new and competing consensus where youth justice and other criminal policy issues were to be brazenly traded in the political marketplace. The *volte face* was as much one of mood and tone as of statute or other new arrangements, and the Labour Party was especially effective in placing the government on the defensive. A series of proposals, many with strong public-order overtones, such as clamping down on 'squeegee merchants' and subjecting children aged under 10 to a 9 o'clock curfew, have kept Labour's tough image on crime to the fore. In May 1996 the Labour Party published *Tackling Youth Crime: Reforming Youth Justice*, in which few punches were pulled. 'Youth crime has been increasing over the last decade – despite government claims to the contrary ... A high proportion of this increase (in recorded crime between 1984 and 1994) relates to car crime and burglary ... It defies belief that while these crimes involving property have risen so dramatically juvenile offending is regarded by the government as dropping' (Labour Party, 1996, p. 2). The document's tone reflected the extent of the recognition that this was an issue upon which the government was vulnerable. For example, 'Far too many youngsters who go through the system stay out of control and persistent young offenders are holding to ridicule the very idea that the law can be enforced' (p. 1). Barely a month after the publication of the Major government's white paper, *Protecting the Public* (which, among other items, proposed mandatory minimum sentences for certain categories of adult offenders), the Labour Party challenged the government's hold on this ground by declaring that 'Ultimately the welfare needs of the young offender cannot outweigh those of the community ... the government appears to have lost sight of this guiding principle ' (Labour Party, 1996, p. 9).

From this brief and preliminary account of the ups and downs of youth justice in England and Wales since the early 1980s, it is evident that a profound transformation has occurred within the political sphere of influence (see Mathiesen, 1996; Rutherford, 1996). It seems likely that significant shifts have also taken place within the media and among criminal justice professional groups. Much work remains to be done to explore the dynamics and inter-relationships of these various spheres over this period, but within two or three years the 'joint moral community', to use Nils Christie's useful concept (Christie, 1993), which had been so crucial during the 1980s, was in a much weakened state. By the mid-1990s there was little on the horizon, notwithstanding the prospect of a Labour government, which promised a turn in the tide.

NOTES

1. The data reviewed in this paragraph address young people under the age of 17, which was the ceiling of the juvenile court's jurisdiction until 1 October 1992. The sentencing provisions of the Criminal Justice Act 1991 which took effect on that date included the replacement of the juvenile court by the youth court which has jurisdiction up to age 18. Tables 3.1–3.3 include 17-year-olds in order to take account of developments since 1992.

2. Much of the early opposition was expressed by senior members of the judiciary, and by some magistrates (a few of whom were reported as resigning in protest). It is interesting to note that two of the senior judicial opposing voices were those of the Lord Chief Justice, Lord Taylor, and Lord Ackner, who three years later were leading opponents of Michael Howard's proposals for mandatory minimum sentences. Pre-dating the intervention of Lord Taylor was the oral evidence of two High Court Justices to the Home Affairs Committee on 17 February 1993 (Home Affairs Select Committee, 1993, pp. 264–70).

3. This trend towards greater severity is evident in the post-1992 data displayed in Tables 3.1–3.3. The total daily number of young people aged under 17 serving custodial sentences in prison department institutions rose from 271 to 417 (a 54 per cent increase) between 30 June 1992 and 30 June 1995. Between 1992–5 the number of defendants of this age group who were remanded to prison service custody rose from 1098 to 1889 (Paul Cavadino, *Recent Statistical Trends in Youth Justice*, Penal Affairs Consortium, May 1996). See also *Trouble-shooter, A Project to Rescue 15 Year Olds from Prison* (London, Howard League for Penal Reform, 1995).

Table 3.1   Number of young people cautioned for indictable offenses
by age, 1984–94

	Males		Females	
	10–14	14–18	10–18	14–18
1984	33,200	44,400	10,400	14,000
1985	34,400	50,900	12,500	18,400
1986	26,300	47,600	8,700	16,300
1987	26,000	53,500	7,500	15,700
1988	22,900	48,600	5,300	13,200
1989	20,300	43,300	4,500	12,200
1990	22,500	52,100	5,900	16,200
1991	21,000	50,500	6,300	17,800
1992	22,500	53,700	8,300	21,200
1993	19,900	48,600	7,500	18,000
1994	19,900	47,900	9,100	18,600

Source: *Criminal Statistics for England and Wales, 1994* (HMSO 1995)
Cm 3010, p. 125.

Table 3.2   Number of young people convicted for indictable offenses
by age, 1984–94

	Males		Females	
	10–14	14–18	10–14	14–18
1984	10,900	83,700	1,000	9,300
1985	9,100	78,200	900	8,900
1986	6,100	63,400	500	6,900
1987	4,300	58,900	300	5,900
1988	3,700	53,600	300	5,600
1989	2,800	40,400	200	4,800
1990	2,600	38,400	200	4,900
1991	2,300	35,100	200	4,400
1992	2,300	31,600	200	4,000
1993	2,300	29,400	200	3,600
1994	2,900	32,700	300	4,400

Source: *Criminal Statistics, England and Wales, 1994* (HMSO, 1995)
Cm 3010, p. 125.

Table 3.3 Number of persons (aged 14–18) sentenced to custody for all offenses and percentage so sentenced for indictable offenses, 1984–94

	Males		Females	
	Number	Per cent	Number	Per cent
1984	12,500	14.4	200	2.5
1985	16,900	14.7	200	2.6
1986	9,200	14.0	200	2.5
1987	8,500	14.0	200	2.5
1988	7,600	13.7	200	2.6
1989	5,600	11.7	100	2.1
1990	4,400	9.5	100	1.7
1991	4,300	9.9	100	1.9
1992	3,900	10.4	100	1.7
1993	3,800	11.1	100	2.6
1994	4,200	11.1	100	2.8

Source: *Criminal Statistics, England and Wales, 1994* (HMSO, 1995) Cm 3010, p. 171.

REFERENCES

Ashworth, A. and Gibson, B. (1994) *The Youth Court, One Year Onwards.* Winchester, England: Waterside.

Christie, N. (1993) *Crime Control as Industry, Towards Gulags Western Style?* London: Routledge.

Clarke, K. (1993) The iron fist in the kid glove for Britain's young offenders. *The Daily Telegraph* (24 February).

Faulkner, D. (1993) All flaws and disorder. *The Guardian* (11 November).

Gelsthorpe, L. and Morris, A. (1994) Juvenile Justice 1945–1992. In M. McGuire *et al.* (Eds.) *The Oxford Handbook of Criminology* (pp. 949–86). Oxford: Oxford University Press.

Heffer, S. (1992) How twice the crime is twice as much reason to play the law and order card. *The Spectator* (15 February).

——. (1993a) Will the force be with him? *The Spectator* (27 March).

——. (1993b) Mr Clarke not only plans to prevent crime, but to prevent criminals too. *The Spectator* (30 May).

Home Affairs Select Committee. (1993) *Juvenile Offenders*, 6th Report, Volume 2: Memoranda of Evidence, Minutes of Evidence and Appendices. London: HMSO.

Labour Party. (1996) *Tackling Youth Crime: Reforming Youth Justice.* A consultation paper on an agenda for change. London: The Labour Party.

Mathiesen, T. (1996) Driving forces behind prison growth: The mass media. *Nordisktidsskrift Kriminalvidenskab* 83, 133–43.

Newburn, T. and Hagell, A. (1994) *Persistent Young Offenders*. London: Policy Studies Institute.

Rutherford, A. (1992) *Growing Out Of Crime*. Winchester, England: Waterside.

——. (1993) *Criminal Justice and the Pursuit of Decency*. Winchester, England: Waterside.

——. (1996) *Transforming Criminal Policy*. Winchester, England: Waterside.

Wade, S. (1996) *The Development of Youth Justice Services in Hampshire, 1987–1991*. M. Phil. dissertation, University of Southampton.

Windlesham, L. (1993) *Responses to Crime, Volume 2, Penal Policy in the Making*. Oxford: Oxford University Press.

4 Juvenile Justice Professionals: Opponents of Reform

Ralph A. Rossum

INTRODUCTION

My argument is straightforward. America's juvenile justice system is failing abysmally, and the burgeoning rate of serious juvenile crime is evidence of this. The failure is exacerbated by demographic trends and the growth of what criminologist John J. DiIulio calls 'moral poverty' (1995, p. 25). At bottom, however, this failure can be traced to systemic defects in America's century-old juvenile justice system; not only has the treatment model on which it is based always been unjust and ineffectual, but it is also wholly incapable of responding to the level of serious and violent juvenile crime the United States is experiencing today and the even higher levels it will experience in the next 10 to 15 years. America's current juvenile justice system – or what I believe is better described as America's 'juvenile injustice system' (Rossum, 1995) – must be fundamentally reformed, but that reform has been and will continue to be stymied by the opposition of those juvenile justice professionals who operate the current system and have a vested interest in its perpetuation.

JUVENILE CRIME AND DEMOGRAPHY

Serious juvenile crime is skyrocketing. Between 1983 and 1992 the number of juveniles arrested for murder rose by 128 per cent, and the number arrested for violent crime rose by 57 per cent. During that same time period, the murder rate for male blacks between the ages of 14 and 17 (76 per cent of whose victims were also black) shot up 320 per cent (Bureau of Justice

Statistics, 1994). During the 1980s the number of arrests for weapons offenses increased 175 per cent among those 12 to 15 years of age, and 133 per cent among all those less than 18 years old (Greenfeld, 1994). During the second half of that decade, delinquency cases generally increased by 16 per cent while the most crime-prone age group in the juvenile population, those between the ages of 14 and 17, fell by approximately 9 per cent (Butts, 1994). Most dramatic was the increase in delinquency cases involving older juveniles and minority juveniles; delinquency cases involving juveniles 17 years of age and older increased by 26 per cent, cases involving minority juveniles 10 to 18 years of age increased by 32 per cent, and cases involving minority juveniles 17 years of age and older increased by 40 per cent. Fully half of all delinquency cases involve crimes serious enough to be listed as FBI Index offenses (Snyder and Sickmund, 1995).

In 1995, juveniles between the ages of 10 and 18 constituted 12.6 per cent of the total US population (Bureau of the Census, 1993). However, according to FBI statistics released in the fall of 1995, they commit 30.9 per cent of all Index offenses, 19.4 per cent of all violent crime and 35.1 per cent of all property crime. More specifically, they commit 16.7 per cent of all murders and non-negligent manslaughters, 15.6 per cent of all aggravated assaults, 16.3 per cent of all forcible rapes, 32.0 per cent of all robberies, 33.4 per cent of all larcenies, 36.2 per cent of all burglaries, and 55.3 per cent of all arsons (Federal Bureau of Investigation, 1995). More individuals are arrested for property crimes at age 16 than at any other age, and more are arrested for crimes of violence at 18 than at any other age (Bureau of Justice Statistics, 1988).

There are many reasons for this increase in serious juvenile crime, and demography is certainly among them. Unlike the decade of the 1980s, when the number of boys in the most crime-prone age group was declining, the number of boys who are 14 to 17 years of age is once again increasing rapidly and will continue to do so.[1] From 1995 to 2005, the number of boys who are 14 to 17 will increase by 16 per cent overall, by 21 per cent for blacks, by 42 per cent for Hispanics and by 55 per cent for Asians; their numbers will increase much faster than the overall US population, which will increase during the same time period by less than 10 per cent. This is not a temporary demographic blip. By 2010, their numbers will increase over the 1995 baseline by 19 per cent overall, by 25 per cent for blacks, by 60 per cent for Hispanics and by 93 per cent for Asians, again outpacing the increase in the overall population of only 14 per cent (see Table 4.1).

What does this increase portend? Birth-cohort studies of all boys born in Philadelphia in 1945 and 1958 have been conducted by Marvin Wolfgang and his associates (Wolfgang *et al.*, 1972; Wolfgang *et al.*, 1987; Tracy *et al.*, 1990).[2] They reveal that about one-third of all boys will have at least one recorded arrest by the time they are 18 – typically when they are between the ages of 14 and 17. More importantly, however, these birth-cohort studies find that approximately 6 per cent of all boys commit five or more crimes before they are 18, and that this chronic offender group accounts for over half of all the serious crimes and about two-thirds of all the violent crimes committed by the entire cohort (Tracy *et al.*, 1990). This '6 per cent do 50 per cent' statistic (DiIulio, 1995, p. 23) has been replicated in longitudinal studies elsewhere in the United States (Hamparian *et al.*, 1978; Shannon, 1988) and in England (Farrington, 1982; West and Farrington, 1973), and provides the basis for predicting with confidence that we are experiencing what criminologist James Alan Fox has termed 'the calm before the crime storm' (Zoglin, 1996, p. 52). As a result of the additional 625 000 boys who will be 14 to 17 years old in the year 2000, there are likely to be over 37 000 more violent criminals on the streets than we have today, each doing five or more crimes before they end their juvenile careers. This grim picture gets worse, for this same '6 per cent do 50 per cent' statistic is likely to mean 73 000 more violent offenders by the year 2005 and 87 000 more by the year 2010. It is little wonder that the US Department of Justice ominously warns in its 1995 report, *Juvenile Offenders and Victims: A National Report*, that juvenile arrests for violent crime will double in the next 15 years (Snyder and Sickmund, 1995).

JUVENILE CRIME AND MORAL POVERTY

In addition to demography, there are other critical reasons for this increase in serious juvenile crime; they include the prevalence of gangs and drug use, the breakdown of the family, and the coarsening of American society, generally resulting in what DiIulio (1995, p. 25) calls the increase of moral poverty. DiIulio defines moral poverty as 'the poverty of growing up surrounded by deviant, delinquent and criminal adults in abusive, violence-ridden, fatherless, Godless and jobless settings'. Moral poverty prevents the inculcation of character in children raised in these desperate circumstances. Character has been defined by James Q. Wilson (1991, p. 5) as empathy and self-control: 'Empathy refers to a willingness to take importantly into account the rights, needs and feelings of others. Self-control refers to a willingness to take importantly into account the more distant consequences of present actions; to be in short somewhat future oriented rather than wholly present oriented.' Character is most commonly and importantly taught to children by their loving and responsible parents. Thus, parents teach empathy and self-control to Tommy when he hits Billy by saying: 'Don't do that; it hurts. You wouldn't like that done to you' (empathy) and 'If you hit him again, you'll be grounded for a week' (self-control prompted by consideration of future consequences).

Without the inculcation of character, children become radically self-regarding. By living for themselves alone and placing 'zero value on the lives of their victims', they become capable of committing the 'most heinous acts of physical violence for the most trivial reasons (e.g., a perception of slight disrespect or the accident of being in their path)' (DiIulio, 1995, p. 26). They also become radically present-oriented. By perceiving no relationship between 'doing right (or wrong) now and being rewarded (or punished) for it later, they live entirely in and for the present moment and quite literally have no concept of the future', resulting in individuals who 'fear neither the stigma of arrest nor the pain of imprisonment' (DiIulio, 1995, p. 26).

The teaching of character is all but impossible in 'fatherless, Godless and jobless' households, and, when character is not taught, the result is crime – often serious and violent crime. (Bennett, DiIulio and Walters, 1996). Among chronically violent offenders, the Bureau of Justice Statistics reports that two-thirds were raised in single-parent households and that 37 per cent had spent some time in a foster home or other childcare institution; over half had parents or foster parents who abused drugs or alcohol; and over 60 per cent had an immediate family member (a father, mother, brother, or sister) with a prison record (Bureau of Justice Statistics, 1993; Greenfeld, 1994). Moral poverty is self-perpetuating; as John DiIulio (1994, p. 25) observes, most of these offenders will 'produce the same sad experience for their children'.

Mark S. Fleisher's ethnographic research of the life trajectories of 194 teenage and young-adult criminals from Washington, Oregon, California, Arizona, and Washington, DC reveals, almost without exception, that these criminals came from families that 'were a social fabric of fragile and undependable social ties that weakly bound children to their parents and other socializers (step-parents, aunts, uncles, cousins, grandparents)' (1995, pp. 248–9). Fleisher further found that nearly all of their parents

> were alcoholics; many used other drugs too, such as marijuana, heroin and cocaine. Many fathers were criminals; often they were drug dealers. Mothers, and sometimes grandmothers too, engaged in criminal activities with their husbands, brothers, sons and nephews. Sometimes these women, the mothers in particular, were passive bystanders, but they always were active consumers of money and goods brought by crime. (p. 248)

Fleisher continues his description of the 'morass of anger and drunkenness and squalid human emotions' in which his subjects were 'enculturated' by noting that the

> parents usually didn't get along well with each other, especially when they were drunk. Husbands beat their wives with fists or slashed them with knives; knife-wielding wives cut their husbands. Fathers and mothers beat their sons and daughters – whipped them with belts, punched them with fists, slapped them and kicked them. (p. 248)

He documented 'numerous' cases of sexual abuse by fathers or by the mothers' boyfriends and reported that many

> mothers of these children were knowing but passive bystanders, pretending not to know, fearful ... that they might be beaten or might have their supply of drugs cut off ... the well-being and criminal pleasures [of these parents invariably came first] ... the children always suffered. (p. 249)

Fleisher concludes that his subjects were raised in conditions of abject moral poverty and that they inevitably 'became like their parents': 'brutal' and 'depraved' – or, as he entitles his book, 'beggars and thieves' (1995, pp. 249, 270). They developed what Fleisher (1995, p. 104) calls a 'defensive worldview' and what James Q. Wilson would call a bad character. Thus, they displayed a feeling of vulnerability and the need to protect themselves, a belief that no-one could be trusted, impulsiveness, insensitivity, a willingness to use violence and intimidation to repel others; a propensity for risk-taking, and a reluctance to become socially intimate.

Serious and violent juvenile crime is increasing, in part, because this kind of moral poverty is increasing. Thus, in 1991, 1.2 million children were born in the United States to unmarried mothers (an illegitimacy rate of 30 per cent); this was up from 665 000 (or a rate of 18.5 per cent) as recently as 1980. During that same time period, the illegitimacy rate for blacks rose from 55 per cent to 68 per cent, for whites from 11 per cent to 22 per cent and for whites with less than a high-school education from 35 per cent to 48 per cent. The illegitimacy rate for white women below the poverty line is 44 per cent, compared with only 6 per cent for white women above the poverty line (Murray, 1993). During the past decade, the incidence of reported child abuse rose by 74 per cent to over 900 000 substantiated cases annually, and the incidence of sexual abuse more than tripled (Snyder and Sickmund, 1995). Moral poverty combines with economic poverty in a most unfortunate fashion, for the rate of child abuse is four times higher in families with incomes of less than $15,000 compared with those with higher incomes, and the rate of neglect is eight times higher (Snyder and Sickmund, 1995). Those who are morally deprived are likely to become criminally depraved, and as moral poverty widens and deepens in this country, there is every reason both to expect and fear what DiIulio (1995, p. 25) calls 'the coming of the super-predators' – his name for 'super crime-prone young males'.

THE PUBLIC CALL FOR PUNISHMENT

When to the consequences of moral poverty are added the demographic consequences of the rapid growth of the most crime-prone age group and the lessons learned from the birth-cohort studies, we see the prospect of an exploding 'demographic crime bomb' (DiIulio, 1995, p. 23), unleashing on the public tens of thousands of morally impoverished juvenile 'super-predators'. The public expects the juvenile justice system to address this issue – to be, as it were, the 'bomb disposal unit' that will defuse or remove this problem. But herein lies the problem: the juvenile justice system is perceived by the public as failing to deal harshly enough with current levels of juvenile crime, to say nothing of what we are likely to experience in the next 10 to 15 years. Thus, when asked in a 1989 Yankelovich Clancy Shulman Poll (Bureau of Justice Statistics, 1991, p. 157) to identify those factors chiefly to blame for teenage violence, 70 per cent of the respondents mentioned 'lenient treatment of juvenile offenders by the courts'; and when asked in the same poll what actions they favored to reduce teenage violence, 79 per cent said 'tougher criminal penalties for juvenile offenders'. Likewise, in a 1996 Gallup Poll (Bureau of Justice Statistics, 1994, p. 179), respondents were told, 'In most places, there are criminal justice programs that treat juveniles differently than adults who commit the same crimes. These programs emphasize protecting and rehabilitating juveniles rather than punishing them,' and were then asked: 'How successful would you say these programs have been at controlling crime?' Nationally, 72 per cent said they were unsuccessful. A 1994 *Los Angeles Times* Poll (Bureau of Justice Statistics, 1994, p. 179) likewise revealed that 68 per cent of all respondents (and 71 per cent of black respondents) believed that juveniles who commit violent crime should 'be treated the same as adults'; only 13 per cent believed they should be 'given more lenient treatment'. The juvenile courts – designed a century ago for a simpler and more innocent era – are regarded by the American public as unable to prevent, and therefore as contributing to, serious juvenile crime. This perception was confirmed for many in September 1993, when four teenagers were arrested for the murder of a British tourist in Florida. All four had been arrested before; in fact, a 13-year-old among them had been previously arrested 15 times on 56 charges and at the time of his first arrest was only 8 years old (Van Gieson, 1993).

The public regards the juvenile courts, and the treatment model on which they are based, as badly in need of fundamental reform. As Paul Johnson (1994, p. A10) notes, the people want juveniles punished for their crimes, and 'they favor punishment that is deterrent and retributive'. One of the most popular reforms with those who favor greater punishment of juveniles is the transfer of serious juvenile offenders to criminal court for trial as an adult. State legislatures have narrowed the jurisdiction of juvenile courts, principally by lowering the age and revising the procedures by which juvenile courts can waive jurisdiction and transfer juveniles to criminal courts; twenty-five states now permit judicial waiver of juveniles to criminal courts at age 14 or younger (Snyder and Sickmund, 1995). Legislatures have also excluded certain offenses (e.g., fifteen states exclude murder and thirteen states exclude crimes of violence) or offense histories (e.g., Ohio excludes felony offenses if the juvenile has a previous criminal conviction) from juvenile court jurisdiction altogether (legislative waiver), and thirteen states have created concurrent jurisdiction, permitting prosecutors to choose whether to proceed in juvenile or criminal court (prosecutorial waiver). These amendments to waiver provisions reflect the wish of legislatures to impose harsher punishments on juvenile perpetrators, although the findings of a study of New York State's revised waiver provisions (Citizens' Committee for Children of New York, 1984) remind us all that a wish is not a fact. It found that there is a tendency for the adult courts to treat defendants who are transferred from juvenile courts as first-time offenders, regardless of the length or seriousness of their juvenile record (which, of course, is sealed and unavailable to the prosecutor or judge). As a consequence, most serious juvenile offenders tried in New York's criminal courts received sanctions less severe than they could have received in the juvenile courts, and only 4 per cent received more severe sanctions than they could otherwise have received (see also Feld, 1983; Tracy *et al.*, 1990; Snyder and Sickmund, 1995).

THE FAILURE OF THE TREATMENT MODEL

Most proposals to make the juvenile justice system more punitive are no more likely to succeed than legislation providing for easier transfer to the criminal courts. This is so, because, at bottom, they do not challenge the 'treatment model' on which the juvenile justice system is predicated and which rejects the very idea of punishment (see Rossum, 1995). Those who established the juvenile justice system in the United States understood juvenile delinquency to be a disease peculiar to childhood. They perceived the purpose of juvenile justice as bringing children into juvenile courts where this disease could be diagnosed by experts and where treatment could be prescribed by a judge to meet the child's individual needs (Ryerson, 1978). The circumstances underlying an act, rather than the act itself, were the court's primary target. Julian Mack, a leading figure in the establishment of America's first juvenile court, summarized these principles in 1909: the state's duty, he wrote, is to discern the physical, mental and moral state of the child to determine whether he is in danger of future criminality. The most important consideration, Judge Mack insisted, 'is not has this boy or girl committed a specific wrong, but what is he, how has he become what he is and what had best be done in his interest and in the interest of the state to save him from a downward career' (1909, p. 119). According to Judge Mack, juvenile court judges 'must be willing and patient enough to search out the underlying causes of the trouble and to formulate the plan by which ... the cure may be effected'. Mack argued that the most serious mistake was to deal with children as criminals, a view he shared with other juvenile court judges (see House Document No. 701, 1904).

Those responsible for establishing America's juvenile justice system wanted juvenile courts to treat delinquents the way pediatric medicine treats children (Rossum, 1995). When children become physically ill, they are not blamed for their misfortune; neither are they stigmatized. Rather, their disease is first diagnosed, and then they are individually treated by medical professionals whose objective is to do what is best for the patient. The children sometimes have to be separated from society if their disease is contagious or to assure the success of their prescribed treatment, but this separation is never punitive in nature. Medical personnel are given maximum discretion to deal with these patients; reliance is placed on their professional training, expertise, ingenuity and goodwill, not on lock-step routines or rigid adherence to rules or regulations.

The juvenile courts were designed to operate on the basis of this same treatment model. Some children contract a disease called juvenile delinquency, but they are no more to be blamed or stigmatized for this misfortune than are their physically stricken counterparts. Instead, juvenile court personnel are to diagnose the nature and cause of the juvenile's disease of delinquency and are to recommend to the juvenile court judge – who is to operate as a physician of sorts – a treatment to be prescribed to address the juvenile's needs. This treatment may require institutionalization, but this separation from society is imposed not as a punishment, but only to ensure the successful treatment of the disease of delinquency and to prevent the spread of the disease to others. And, just as a physician has the discretion to do what is necessary to save his patients, so, too, the juvenile court judge is to be authorized, by the purpose clause of the juvenile court's enabling legislation, to do whatever is 'in the best interest of the child'.

The juvenile justice system was thus designed to depart from the traditional court of law in almost every respect. The juvenile court was to be an institution where behavioral specialists could meet in order to assist children and to publicize and rectify the complex problems underlying juvenile delinquency. Its principal concerns were the child's character, psychology, and home environment. Its mission was to remove young offenders from criminal courts and provide them with the care and supervision typical of that found in a stable and loving family. Since those who established the juvenile court assumed that the interests of the state, of delinquent children, and of their families were identical, they eliminated the adversarial atmosphere of criminal courts and, along with it, the procedural safeguards of due process. They replaced the cold, objective standards of criminal procedure with informal procedures, based on *parens patriae*.

They even developed a specialized vocabulary in which petitions of delinquency replaced criminal complaints, hearings replaced trials, adjudications of delinquency replaced judgments of guilt, and dispositions replaced sentences. The public was excluded from juvenile hearings, to protect children further from the public stigma of a criminal prosecution. Finally, judges were granted broad discretion to adjudicate delinquency and set dispositions. The principle underlying the juvenile justice system was to combine flexible decision-making with individualized intervention to treat and rehabilitate offenders rather than to punish offenses. Juvenile courts, therefore, were expected to be informal and offender-oriented.[3]

Evidence is increasingly mounting that the fundamental problems confronting America's juvenile justice system stem from the very treatment model on which it is based (Kramer, 1993). The treatment model's focus on the offender rather than on the offense contributes to the public's accurate perception that the juvenile courts are unjustifiably lenient. This is so because the treatment model prohibits juvenile courts from linking the seriousness of the offense to the subsequent treatment they prescribe. In juvenile court, a juvenile who commits murder is not charged with, found guilty of, or punished for murder; rather, he is simply adjudicated delinquent and treated in such a way as to cure his disease of delinquency. His murderous conduct is a symptom of his disease of delinquency and of his need for individually tailored treatment to cure him of that disease. So, too, for a juvenile who shoplifts; his misdeed establishes him as a delinquent – no more and no less than the one who murders – and shows him to be equally in need of individualized treatment to cure his disease. How long the treatment of these two juveniles should continue and how coercive the intervention should be (for example, whether it should be probation as opposed to confinement in a secure detention facility) are determined not by what they have done but by what the juvenile court judge believes is necessary to cure them of their disease of delinquency. By individualizing treatment in this way and by focusing on the juvenile's disease rather than on his victim's anguish, pain, or loss, the juvenile court obscures any relationship between an act and its consequences. The juvenile offender is neither forced to confront the consequences of what he has done to others (a lesson in empathy) nor made to understand that what is being done to him is a consequence of his criminal offense (a lesson in self-control). Furthermore, by characterizing dispositions as treatment rather than punishment and by closing its proceedings to the public, it prevents the threat of punishment from being communicated to other potential offenders and thereby further erodes the general deterrent value of its sanctions (Rossum, 1996).

The treatment model also results in a great deal of injustice in the juvenile justice system (McCarthy, 1977; Rubin, 1979; Sampson and Laub, 1993). By adhering to the model and focusing only on the offender, the juvenile courts violate the principles of equality (that like cases should be treated alike) and proportionality (that the severity of the sanction should be proportionate to the seriousness of the offense) and produce disparate results based on such irrelevant offender characteristics as race and sex. Juvenile-court judges, possessing vast discretion, often impose dispositions of community-based counseling and supervision on white juveniles who have committed serious crimes of violence but who are considered amenable to treatment because they come from intact, middle-class families living in good neighborhoods; at the same time, they repeatedly confine for years in secure detention facilities black juveniles who have committed minor property offenses but who are diagnosed as incorrigible and unamenable to treatment because they come from single-parent households or impoverished neighborhoods. As Sampson and Laub (1993, pp. 304–6) report in their multivariate regression analysis of data from more than 200 US counties, for all categories of offenses (i.e. personal, property, or drug-related), black juveniles are significantly more likely than white juveniles to be placed in secure predisposition detention and to be adjudicated to 'out-of-home placement'.

JUVENILE JUSTICE REFORM AND THE JUSTICE MODEL

These criticisms, together with the growing realization that the juvenile justice system is a century-old institution 'installed at a time when delinquents were known more for stealing bicycles than shooting bystanders' (Danzinger, 1993, A14) and hence hopelessly ill-equipped to deal with late-twentieth-century violent juvenile predators, have led thoughtful critics to call for fundamental juvenile justice reform based on what has been called the 'justice model' (von Hirsch, 1976).[4] Critics such as the Institute of Judicial Administration and the American Bar Association (jointly, they drafted 23 volumes of juvenile justice standards) and the Twentieth Century Fund (through its Task Force on Sentencing Policy Toward Young Offenders) argue that the informal, offender-oriented treatment model must be replaced with a formal, offense-oriented model based on the principles of equality and proportionality.[5] Such a model seeks to hold both juveniles responsible for their criminal misdeeds and the juvenile justice system accountable to the public for what it does to these juveniles; Feld (1984; 1993) has called such reforms the 'criminalizing of juvenile justice'.

The justice model pursues individual responsibility by linking dispositions closely to delinquent acts (future orientation) and by utilizing dispositions, such as restitution, that encourage juveniles to recognize their obligations to the community and to the victims of their criminal acts (empathy). By so doing, it teaches character to juveniles raised in moral poverty. It pursues system accountability through its insistence that dispositions must be limited, deserved, uniform, and justified. To ensure that similarly situated offenders are treated similarly and that the most serious offenders receive the most punitive sanctions, it relies on the use of presumptive and determinate dispositions where the disposition in any case depends upon the nature and seriousness of the criminal offense, the age of the offender, and the number, recency, and seriousness of any prior offenses. This, in turn, inculcates self-control by teaching juveniles that they will be held responsible for their criminal acts; that the more serious and frequent their acts, the more responsible they will be held; and that the older they are, the more responsible they will be expected to be. Also, consistent with accountability, the justice model provides the public with the opportunity to scrutinize the performance of juvenile courts through its requirements that all hearings and all records (other than the juvenile's social file) be open to the public (Rossum, 1995).

We are witnessing in the United States a public repudiation of the treatment model. It is unjust in application, in that it results in inequality and disproportionality. It is unsuccessful in practice, as soaring rates of serious juvenile crime attest. We are also witnessing a yearning for, and inchoate articulation of, the justice model; this is apparent both in the calls for greater punishment of serious and violent juvenile crime (implicit here is an attempt to focus on the offense rather than the offender) and in the public's renewed interest in issues of character. The treatment model fails to teach character to juvenile offenders, in that it obscures any relationship between an act and its consequences. As I have argued elsewhere,

> If character is defined as empathy and self-control, the juvenile courts, as presently constituted, not only fail to teach character but may also be said to lack character themselves. By taking into account only the rights, needs and feelings of the offender, they ignore his offense and fail to display empathy for the rights, needs and feelings of his victims. And, by taking into account only the offender's disease of delinquency, his status as the victim of that disease, and their professional interest in restoring him to that state of emotional and psychological health he would be enjoying had he not succumbed to that disease, they display a present-orientation – their goal is to restore him to what they imagine he would have been, not to prepare him for what he can become. (Rossum, 1996, p. 838)

There is a growing perception that parents can teach character to their children not only through the examples they set and the rules they impose but also by the books they read aloud to them, and the result has been the prolonged elevation to bestseller status of William Bennett's *The Book of Virtues*. There is also the recognition, however, that many parents – themselves morally impoverished – are incapable of teaching character and that other institutions, most notably the public schools, must substitute for them; one consequence of this has been the widespread introduction of character-education programs into the public schools (Heath, 1994; Lickona, 1991). Another consequence has been the recognition that character can also be taught (or at least its principles reinforced) by the juvenile courts, but only if they abandon the treatment model and adopt the justice model in its place. Adoption of the justice model is opposed, however, by those who actually operate the current failed juvenile justice system and have a vested interest in preserving the status quo. Survey research explains why: juvenile justice professionals, many of whom are influential in state politics and effective in testifying before their state legislatures, oppose any efforts to limit their discretion and hold them more accountable for their actions.

OPPOSITION OF JUVENILE JUSTICE PROFESSIONALS TO THE JUSTICE MODEL

As part of a research project funded by the US Department of Justice for which I was the principal investigator, Christopher Manfredi of McGill University and I conducted a national survey of juvenile justice professionals to gauge their attitudes toward juvenile justice reform (Rossum, Koller and Manfredi, 1987). The survey's 8 355 respondents were nationally distributed, with each state's portion of the sample closely approximating its percentage of the US population. They included 792 legal professionals (i.e., judges and attorneys), 679 probation officers, 594 social service employees, 3331 law enforcement officers and 2959 other professionals (including 719 criminal justice professors and researchers, 432 correctional officers, 247 justice planners, 200 juvenile court personnel and 92 state legislators) (see Rossum, 1995, for earlier published results from this survey).

The questionnaire itself consisted of 74 substantive questions, 39 of which concerned attitudes and policy preferences. Three questions asked respondents to indicate their perception of juvenile crime as a problem and to evaluate how well it has been dealt with compared to other problems. The questionnaire also asked respondents to evaluate the performance of seven organizations and institutions involved in juvenile issues, including juvenile courts, state legislatures, and the police. The survey data reveal juvenile justice professionals fully appreciate the problems caused by moral poverty: only 31 per cent of the sample agreed that 'parents are doing a good job raising their children'. The data also reveal that, although 91 per cent of the respondents believe that juvenile crime is a serious problem, 86 per cent believe it is becoming more serious, and 78 per cent believe it is being dealt with more poorly than other social problems, they remain resistant to change and insist on keeping intact the juvenile court's informal, discretionary decision-making.

Among the various professional groups represented in the sample, law-enforcement personnel, who would benefit from the more predictable decision-making that a formal, rules-driven system would foster, displayed the most interest in the justice model. Thus, 82 per cent of law-enforcement personnel support victim impact statements before sentencing, 80 per cent favor mandatory minimum sentences for certain offenses, 78 per cent would allow the adult criminal justice system to have access to juvenile court records and 75 per cent would mandate prosecutor participation in all decisions after the initial apprehension. Additionally, 76 per cent of law-enforcement personnel reject the contention that juvenile crime is more the responsibility of society than of the individual offender, and 72 per cent disagree that social services and counseling are the best responses to juvenile crime. Law-enforcement personnel also tend to view juvenile crime as a more serious problem than do the other professional groups, and see it as being dealt with poorly by the juvenile courts and by state legislatures (see Table 4.2).

By contrast, legal professionals (i.e. lawyers who practice in juvenile court and juvenile court judges), probation officers, and social services personnel continue to embrace the treatment model. This is not surprising, as they have the most to lose if juvenile courts become more formalized, thereby reducing their discretion. Thus, among social services personnel, 73 per cent favor diverting juvenile misdemeanants from the courtroom experience to community service, 64 per cent believe that punishment is an inappropriate element of juvenile justice, 58 per cent believe increased funding of social services reduces juvenile crime, and 51 per cent believe that social services and counseling are the best responses to crime. Among legal professionals, 75 per cent oppose limiting the discretion exercised by judges in sentencing decisions, 65 per cent defend the emphasis that juvenile courts put on rehabilitation, 60 per cent favor the use of indeterminate sentences, 57 per cent oppose setting mandatory minimum penalties for certain offenses, and 55 per cent favor diverting juvenile misdemeanants to community service. Among probation officers, 65 per cent oppose permitting school principals access to the juvenile court legal records of their students, 61 per cent defend the current juvenile courts' emphasis on rehabilitation and favor diverting juvenile misdemeanants to community service, 58 per cent favor the use of indeterminate sentences, and 53 per cent believe that the courtroom relationship between the state and the juvenile need not necessarily be adversarial. All three of these groups also tend to believe that the problem of juvenile crime is not too serious and is being effectively addressed.

These findings are consistent with what other scholars have learned from research on the attitudes of juvenile justice professionals conducted in such diverse jurisdictions as San Diego County, Kansas, Illinois, Minnesota, and Washington State (see Ariessohn, 1972; Arnold 1975; Schumacher and Anderson, 1979; Kittel, 1983; and Schneider and Schramm, 1986). For example, Kittel (1983) found in his study of juvenile court judges in Minnesota, that when asked to decide a hypothetical case, only one judge in five chose an accountability-oriented disposition. Juvenile justice professionals are eager to protect their discretion and are often politically skilled and well-positioned to protect their interests. Examples of this can be found in the serious juvenile offender statutes passed in the following eight states: California, Colorado, Delaware, Georgia, Kentucky, Illinois, New York, and North Carolina. On a superficial level, these laws seem to be offense-oriented and therefore appear to promote individual responsibility; they single out serious and violent offenders for differential and less rehabilitative treatment, handling them within the juvenile court's own jurisdiction and imposing on them sanctions based on the seriousness of their offenses (Forst *et al.*, 1985). On a more fundamental level, however, these laws do less to advance the interests of either individual responsibility or system accountability than they do to preserve the discretion of juvenile justice professionals. They restrict the application of the principles of responsibility and accountability to serious offenders only, thereby preserving the traditional informality and discretionary decision-making of the treatment model in all other cases. Not surprisingly, the National Council of Juvenile and Family Court Judges (NCJFCJ), the professional association of juvenile court judges, has endorsed such statutes and lobbied and testified on their behalf, as they pose no real threat to their judicial discretion. The NCJFCJ viewed these statutes as an acceptable and necessary concession to state legislators, under mounting public pressure to reform juvenile justice. However, in a special issue of its national journal devoted to serious juvenile offenders, the NCJFCJ made clear its continued opposition to true accountability-based reforms by declaring defiantly that 'proposals which would materially and adversely alter traditional individualized rehabilitative models and treatment philosophies of the juvenile justice system are unacceptable. Juvenile justice resources should accordingly primarily continue to be directed toward individualized treatment' (National Council of Juvenile and Family Court Judges, 1984).

CONCLUSION

It is the unwillingness of juvenile court judges and other juvenile justice professionals to relinquish their discretion and to account publicly for their actions that stands in the way of fundamental reform. The discretion they cumulatively exercise is vast. In closed proceedings, where they are free from procedural rules and shielded from the harsh light of public scrutiny, they annually handle approximately 1.5 million delinquency cases, 725 000 of which are serious enough to be classified as UCR Index Offenses. Of this number, they will informally dismiss or divert 49 per cent of them, including 30 per cent of crimes of violence (defined by the UCR as criminal homicides, forcible rapes, robberies, and aggravated assaults) and 51 per cent of crimes against property (defined by the UCR as burglaries, larceny-thefts, motor-vehicle thefts, and arsons). Of the 51 per cent that they formally handle, they will subsequently dismiss 21 per cent before adjudication and waive one per cent to the criminal courts. Of the 29 per cent they actually adjudicate, they will place 17 per cent on probation, place 8 per cent in detention, and dismiss or otherwise dispose of the remaining 4 per cent (Snyder and Sickmund, 1995). Of the 8 per cent they place in detention, they will confine the 2 per cent who have committed crimes of violence for an average of 353 days, the 4 per cent who have committed property crimes for an average of 217 days, and the remaining 2 per cent who have committed primarily drug or public order offenses for an average of 150 days. (These figures derived from data found in Snyder and Sickmund, 1995 and Butts, 1994.)

These very low detention rates and the brief periods of confinement for the few who are detained certainly do not teach empathy and self-control to those burgeoning numbers of young males in the most crime-prone age group whose character is not being shaped at home or in school; after all, nationwide in any given year, for all those juveniles arrested by the police and then actually referred to the juvenile court for their offenses (half of which, to repeat, will be serious enough to be classified as Index Offenses), the average detention imposed by the juvenile court will be only 20 days (Rossum, 1996).[6] An average anticipated sanction of 20 days for the approximately 12 per cent[7] of all juvenile offenders unlucky enough actually to be both arrested by the police and referred to the juvenile court for their offense (or more likely, simply for their last offense) suggests to these juveniles that they are largely immune to the law's force and sanctions. An average of 20 days does not reinforce for them the principle that the law means what it says and says what it means; but it certainly confirms the public's perception that the juvenile courts are far too lenient and its conclusion that the current juvenile justice system is a quaint, turn-of-the-last-century institution whose time is long since past. An average of 20 days of detention is not a sanction likely to instill fear in the hearts of today's run-of-the-mill juvenile offenders, to say nothing of tomorrow's juvenile 'super-predators'. It reveals the high cost that juvenile justice professionals are already imposing on the public as they resist replacing the outmoded treatment model (and the discretion it provides them) with the justice model, and it suggests how much higher that cost is likely to become when that volatile mixture of demography and moral poverty explodes in the coming years.

Table 4.1   Increases in the Size of the Most Crime-Prone Age Group from 1995 to 2010 (boys 14–17 years of age)

| | (Numbers in thousands) | | | | |
	Overall	Whites	Blacks	Hispanics	Asians
1995	7,503	5,952	1,163	933	304
2000	8,129	6,394	1,241	1,078	397
increase since 1995	626 8.3%	442 7.4%	78 6.7%	145 15.6%	93 30.1%
increase of entire group since 1995	4.9%	3.6%	7.1%	16.3%	24.3%
2005	8,716	6,734	1,403	1,327	472
increase since 1995	1,213 16.2%	782 13.1%	240 20.6%	394 42.2%	168 55.3%
increase of entire group since 1995	9.4%	6.9%	14.1%	33.2%	49.7%
2010	8,949	6,805	1,458	1,493	588
increase over 1995	1,446 19.3%	853 14.3%	295 25.4%	560 60.0%	284 93.4%
increase of entire group since 1995	14.0%	10.1%	21.4%	51.2%	76.2%

Source: Bureau of the Census, 1993

Table 4.2   Mean Response by Profession

Variable	Legal	Probation	Social Services	Law Enforcement	Others
Seriousness*	7.73	8.11	8.07	8.25	8.03
How well dealt with**	4.07	4.27	4.02	3.60	3.80
Legislative performance#	2.74	2.82	2.90	2.60	2.76
Performance of juvenile courts#	3.82	3.96	3.69	3.17	3.49

* 10-point scale: 'not serious' to 'very serious'
** 10-point scale: 'poorly' to 'well'
# 6-point scale: 'poor' to 'good'

NOTES

1. Crime by girls is a growing but modest problem. Girls are responsible for only about nine per cent of all juvenile murders and 13 per cent of all juvenile violent crime, and they have recidivism rates of 20 per cent as opposed to 46 per cent for boys (Snyder and Sickmund, 1995).
2. Included in the birth cohorts were all boys born in Philadelphia in the target year and who continually resided in the city at least from their tenth through eighteenth birthdays. There were 9945 boys in the 1945 cohort and 13 160 boys in the 1958 cohort (Tracy *et al.*, 1990; Wolfgang *et al.*, 1972).
3. Beginning with *In re Gault*, 387 US 1 (1967), the United States Supreme Court has sought to formalize the procedures of juvenile courts while keeping them offender-oriented. In *Gault*, the Court proclaimed that 'under our Constitution, the condition of being a boy does not justify a kangaroo court' and held that juveniles are constitutionally entitled to such due process protections enjoyed by adults as notice of charges, representation by counsel, confrontation and cross-examination of witnesses, and the privilege against self-incrimination. Writing for the majority, Justice Abe Fortas argued that 'the absence of substantive standards has not necessarily meant that children receive careful, compassionate, individualized treatment'. The Court's objective was to legalize the adjudicative phase of delinquency proceedings without affecting, and certainly without questioning the

justice of, the juvenile court's emphasis on individualized rehabilitation in other areas and proceedings. This objective has continued to guide the Court in subsequent cases. Thus, it required in *In re Winship*, 397 US 358 (1970), that delinquency must be proved beyond a reasonable doubt and in *Breed* v. *Jones*, 421 US 519 (1975), that waiver hearings must precede adjudication hearings. On the other hand, it found in *McKeiver* v. *Pennsylvania*, 403 US 528 (1971), that juveniles do not possess the right to jury trials and in *Fare* v. *Michael* C., 422 US 707 (1979), that a juvenile's request to speak to a probation officer does not invoke Fifth Amendment protections under *Miranda* v. *Arizona*, 384 US 436 (1966). In each of these cases, the Court sought to preserve the delicate balance between what it called in *Schall* v. *Martin,* 467 US 253, 263 (1984), 'the informality and flexibility' that it believed is necessary for rehabilitation and 'the "fundamental fairness" demanded by the Due Process Clause'. Demonstrating in still another policy arena the judiciary's institutional incapacity to resolve complex policy questions, it was unaware that the higher procedural standards it was mandating would impair the rehabilitative mission of the juvenile courts (Horowitz, 1977).

4.   See von Hirsch (1976), in which he argued that just deserts, rather than deterrence, incapacitation, or rehabilitation, should serve as the primary justification for punishment. Von Hirsch argued that specific punishments should be imposed on offenders according to the principle of commensurate deserts. Sentences should be determined by the seriousness of an offense and the number and seriousness of prior convictions, rather than by the potential utility of sentences in crime prevention. Von Hirsch also proposed that a sentencing policy based on commensurate deserts should contain five components: (1) presumptive sentences should replace indeterminate sentences; (2) sentencing guidelines should be adopted in which the relative seriousness of various offenses and their corresponding sentences are specified; (3) the number and seriousness of prior offenses should be related more directly to increases in the severity of the presumptive sentence for each offense; (4) judges should have the option to order sentences above or below the presumptive sentence, but only within a prescribed range and under specified circumstances; and (5) sentencing guidelines should include general principles of aggravation and mitigation. See also von Hirsch (1985, 1993); and American Friends Service Committee (1971).

5.   The IJA-ABA's 23 volumes of juvenile justice standards rejected any *parens patriae* justification for intervention into juveniles' lives, advocated procedural formality in juvenile court proceedings, and recommended determinate dispositions regulated by the requirements of equality and proportionality. The IJA-ABA standards also called for reductions in judicial discretion and larger roles for both prosecutors and defense attorneys (see Flicker, 1977). The Twentieth Century Fund Task Force concluded that the principles of culpability and

proportionality, along with traditional concepts of diminished responsibility according to age, should guide sentencing decisions (Twentieth
Century Fund Task Force, 1978). The State of Washington has,
in fact, adopted such a formal, offense-oriented juvenile justice system. See Schneider and Schramm (1986) and Rossum, Koller and
Manfredi (1987).

6.   An average anticipated sanction of 20 days was derived as follows:
In 1992, the juvenile courts received 743 700 delinquency petitions;
in 8 per cent (or 59 500) of these cases, the juvenile court detained the
juveniles involved to a period of confinement. (Snyder and Sickmund,
1995, pp. 132, 134.) In 2 per cent (or 14 875) of these cases, the juveniles had committed violent offenses and received an average period
of confinement of 353 days; in 4 per cent (or 29 750) of these cases,
they had committed property offenses and received an average period
of confinement of 217 days; and in another 2 per cent (or 14 875) of
the cases, they had committed drug or public order offenses and
received an average period of confinement of 150 days. The total
length of confinement for all 743 700 juveniles referred to juvenile
court was 15 425 375 days, or an average length of confinement of
20 days.

7.   The figure of 12 per cent was derived as follows: Nationally, only
20 per cent of all crimes (including only 21 per cent of all Index
Offenses) are cleared by arrest (Bureau of Justice Statistics, 1988,
p. 68). Assuming that juvenile crime is cleared at the same rate as
adult crime, then only 20 per cent of juvenile offenders are arrested for
their offenses, and, since only 60 per cent of those juveniles who are
arrested are subsequently referred to juvenile courts (figure derived
from data presented in Snyder and Sickmund, 1995, pp. 100, 126), the
percentage of juveniles who commit offenses who are actually referred
to juvenile court drops to 12 per cent (60 per cent of the 20 per cent).

REFERENCES

American Friends Service Committee. (1971) *Struggle for Justice*. New York:
Wang and Hill.

Ariessohn, R. (1972) Offense v. offender in juvenile court. *Juvenile Justice*
23, 17–32.

Arnold, W. (1975) Grass roots justice in middle America: The county courts
in Kansas. *Kansas Journal of Sociology* 11, 16–31.

Bennett, W. J., DiIulio, J. and Walters, J. P. (1996) *Body Count: Moral
Poverty ... and How to Win America's War Against Crime and Drugs*.
New York: Simon & Schuster.

Bureau of the Census. (1993) *Projections of the Population, by Age, Sex,
Race and Hispanic Origin, for the United States: 1993 to 2050, Middle
Series*. Washington, DC: US Department of Commerce.

Bureau of Justice Statistics. (1988) *Report to the Nation on Crime and Justice: The Data*. 2nd edition. Washington, DC: US Department of Justice.
——. (1991) *Sourcebook of Criminal Justice Statistics – 1990*. Edited by T. J. Flanagan and K. Maguire. Washington, DC: US Department of Justice.
——. (1993) *Survey of State Prison Inmates, 1991*. Washington, DC: US Department of Justice.
——. (1994) *Sourcebook of Criminal Justice Statistics – 1993*. Edited by K. Maguire and A. L. Pastore. Washington, DC: US Department of Justice.
Butts, J. A. (1994) *Juvenile Court Statistics 1991*. Pittsburgh, PA.: National Center for Juvenile Justice.
Citizens' Committee for Children of New York. (1984) *The Experiment that Failed: The New York Juvenile Offender Law – A Study Report*. New York: Citizens' Committee for Children of New York.
Danzinger, J. (1993) Children who murder. *Wall Street Journal* (7 April), A14.
DiIulio, J. J. (1994) The question of black crime. *The Public Interest* (Fall), 3–32.
——. (1995) The coming of the super-predators. *The Weekly Standard* (27 November), 23–8.
Farrington, David P. (1982) Longitudinal analyses of criminal violence. In M. E. Wolfgang and N. A. Weiner (eds.), *Criminal Violence* (pp. 171–200). Beverly Hills, California: Sage Publications.
Federal Bureau of Investigation. (1995) *Crime in the United States: 1994*. Washington, DC: US Department of Justice.
Feld, B. C. (1983) Delinquent careers and criminal policy: Just deserts and the waiver decision. *Criminology* 23, 195–212.
——. (1984) Criminalizing juvenile justice: Rules of procedure for the juvenile court. *Minnesota Law Review* 69, 141–276.
——. (1993) Criminalizing the American juvenile court. In M. Tonry and N. Morris (eds.), *Crime and Justice: An Annual Review of Research* 17 (pp. 197–237). Chicago: University of Chicago Press.
Fleisher, M. S. (1995) *Beggars and Thieves: Lives of Urban Street Criminals*. Madison, Wisconsin: University of Wisconsin Press.
Flicker, B. D. (1977) *Standards for Juvenile Justice: A Summary and Analysis*. Cambridge, Massachusetts: Ballinger Publishing Company.
Forst, Martin L., *et al.* (1985) Indeterminate and determinate sentencing of juvenile delinquents: A national survey of approaches to commitment and release decision-making. *Juvenile and Family Court Journal* 36, 10–25.
Greenfeld, L. A. (1994) Youth violence and the backgrounds of chronic violent offenders. Paper presented at the Institute of United States Studies conference on Juvenile Justice and the Limits of Social Policy, University of London, England, (9 May).
Hamparian, D. M., Schuster, R., Dinitz, S. and Conrad, J. P. (1978) *The Violent Few: A Study of Dangerous Juvenile Offenders*. Lexington, Massachusetts: DC Heath.
Heath, D. H. (1994) *Schools of Hope: Developing Mind and Character in Today's Youth*. San Francisco: Jossey-Bass Publishers.

Horowitz, D. L. (1977) *The Courts and Social Policy*. Washington, DC: Brookings Institution Press.

House Document No. 701. (1904) *Children's Courts in the United States: Their Origin, Development and Results*. 58th Congress., 2nd Session.

Johnson, P. (1994) Crime: The people want revenge. *Wall Street Journal* (4 January), A10.

Kramer, R. (1993) The assault on juvenile crime. *Wall Street Journal* (8 November), A16.

Kittel, N. G. (1983) Juvenile justice philosophy in Minnesota. *Juvenile and Family Court Journal* 34, 93–108.

Lickona, T. (1991) *Educating for Character: How Our Schools Can Teach Respect and Responsibility*. New York: Bantam.

Mack, J. (1909) The juvenile court. *Harvard Law Review* 23, 104–30.

McCarthy, F. (1977) Should juvenile delinquency be abolished? *Crime and Delinquency* 23, 196–203.

Murray, C. (1993) The coming white underclass. *Wall Street Journal* (29 October), A12.

National Council of Juvenile and Family Court Judges. (1984) The juvenile court and serious offenders: 38 recommendations. *Juvenile and Family Court Journal* 35, 1–16.

Rossum, R. A. (1995) Holding juveniles accountable: Reforming America's 'juvenile injustice system'. *Pepperdine Law Review* 22, 907–31.

——. (1996) Reforming juvenile justice and improving juvenile character: The case for the justice model. *Pepperdine Law Review* 23, 823–40.

Rossum, R. A., Koller, B. J. and Manfredi, C. P. (1987) *Juvenile Justice Reform: A Model for the States*. Claremont, California: Rose Institute.

Rubin, H. T. (1979) Retain the juvenile court? Legislative developments, reform directions and the call for abolition. *Crime and Delinquency* 25, 281–98.

Ryerson, E. (1978) *The Best-Laid Plans: America's Juvenile Court Experiment*. New York: Wang and Hill.

Sampson, R. J. and Laub, J. H. (1993) Structural variations in juvenile court processing: Inequality, the underclass and social control. *Law & Society Review* 27, 285–311.

Schneider, A. and Schramm, D. (1986) The Washington state juvenile justice system reform: A review of findings. *Criminal Justice Policy Review* 1, 211–31.

Schumacher, R. and Anderson, D. (1979) An attitude factor in juvenile court decisionmaking. *Juvenile and Family Court Journal* 31, 31–46.

Shannon, L. W. (1988) *Criminal Career Continuity: Its Social Context*. New York: Human Sciences Press.

Snyder, H. N. and Sickmund, M. (1995) *Juvenile Offenders and Victims: A National Report*. Washington, DC: Office of Juvenile Justice and Delinquence Prevention, US Department of Justice.

Tracy, P. E., Wolfgang, M. E. and Figlio, R. M. (1990) *Delinquency Careers in Two Birth Cohorts*. New York: Plenum Press.

Twentieth Century Fund Task Force. (1978) *Confronting Youth Crime*. New York: Holmes and Meier Publishers, Inc.

Van Gieson, J. C. (1993) Boys held in slaying of tourist. *The Orlando Sentinel* (6 October), A1.

von Hirsch, A. (1976). *Doing Justice: The Choice of Punishments.* New York: Wang and Hill.

——. (1985) *Past or Future Crimes.* New Brunswick, New Jersey: Rutgers University Press.

——. (1993) *Censure and Sanctions.* Oxford, England: Oxford University Press.

West, D. J. and Farrington, D. P. (1973) *Who Becomes Delinquent?* London: Heinemann.

Wilson, James Q. (1991) *On Character.* Washington, DC: The A.E.I. Press.

Wolfgang, M. E., Figlio, R. M. and Sellin, T. (1972) *Delinquency in a Birth Cohort.* Chicago: University of Chicago Press.

Wolfgang, M. E., Thornberry, T. P. and Figlio, R. M. (1987) *From Boy to Man, From Delinquency to Crime.* Chicago: University of Chicago Press.

Zoglin, R. (1996) Now for the bad news: A teenage time bomb. *Time* (January 15), 52–5.

5 Common Sense and Juvenile Justice in America
Edwin Meese III

INTRODUCTION

Too often discussions of crime degenerate into debates about punishment versus social causes, or sociological theories versus legal minutiae. In thinking about juvenile crime especially, it is important to avoid such pointless debates and focus on the fact that juvenile crime is a complex problem that defies easy solution. There are simply no panaceas or quick and inexpensive fixes. One of the great misfortunes in dealing with this very serious problem is that many politicians approach the subject in exactly that way, as though there are easy answers. In light of this, it is very important to keep in mind that there is a definite nexus between dependent children – those who have been neglected and abused – and delinquent children. One thing that has been pointed out by such commentators as William J. Bennett and James Q. Wilson is that a good part of the problem of criminal justice is not amenable to governmental solutions. In this regard, moral values and an emphasis on family and parenting are critical to any long-term solution.

We should recognize that there are ways in which government policies in these areas can be improved. It is crucial that unintended disincentives to the kind of moral values that are essential to family stability be checked; as a result, the criminal justice system, and particularly the juvenile justice system, needs to be made more effective. One of the facts of life that has been true in the past and continues to be true is that we are in short supply of resources. Therefore, we must pursue ways of thinking about how we can use our limited resources in more fruitful ways.

In this regard it may be particularly helpful to distinguish between the casual juvenile offender and the persistent, committed offender, and to recognize the dual roles of the juvenile court and the juvenile justice system generally in dealing with them. Such a realistic view of the situation sees the function of the juvenile court as seeking to advance the best interests of the minor while simultaneously protecting the safety of society. Both of these objectives can be best served if at the earliest stage the casual offender or the first-time offender is taken out of the system entirely, hopefully never to return. In a sense, such an approach gives a one hundred per cent return on investment in a crime-prevention program, because the person who has already demonstrated by at least one or two acts that they would easily fall into a life of crime is taken out of that world and prevented from going further: a tremendous advantage as far as society is concerned. This approach does not flinch at the fact that we have to recognize that there are other types of persistent, committed offenders who must be dealt with in very different ways.

There are a couple of things in the profile of the serious habitual offender which has been developed by the Office of Juvenile Justice and Delinquency Prevention in the United States that bear repeating. The first is that the serious habitual offender, in the United States at least, after first becoming involved with the law remains the focus of the attention of the criminal justice system for about 12 years of increasingly serious criminal behavior until he is finally incarcerated as a so-called 'career' criminal. It is also true that this serious habitual offender is likely to be one in 30 of his type who will commit murder sometime after release from a state prison. One out of 60 actually commit murder within five years of their release from state prison. A particularly important conclusion about serious habitual offenders is that, even after repeated incarcerations or after repeated brushes with the law, this offender often does not consider that what he has done is all that bad; after all, the authorities never really did anything about what he should do or about what he has done. He has found out that, for much of that 12-year history, the system hardly noticed what he did, no matter what it was, unless it was at the level of murder or something comparably serious.

When nothing is done, or when the person feels that he has beaten the system – and I use the word 'he' because we know that the vast majority of the serious habitual offenders are male – we have in effect told that person that they have beaten the system. One of the things we have to recognize is that, short of incarceration, at least in the United States, when that person comes backs to the neighborhood and back to the gang, it is most likely that it will appear to the culprit as well as those around him that he beat the system again; this will be the case unless there is some clear-cut indication that he is in fact being punished. This is a factor that cannot be ignored when we look at the variations of intermediate treatment and how they are interpreted in the society in which the young offender is living. It is usually the case that he has been negatively conditioned by the system itself to continue his bad conduct. Very aggressive behavior traits often signal trouble at an early age, but the system did not react, often because of an inability to figure out a punishment or a treatment mode that is actually going to arrest this type of behavior. As a result, all too often the system deals with particular individuals in inconsistent, contradictory and often counter-productive ways.

In talking about the serious habitual offenders who are very dangerous even though they happen to be juveniles, it is important to recognize that the number in each community is not large. In the United States the serious habitual offender is a category which is roughly four-tenths of 1 per cent of the 14- to 17-year-old population. But for every serious habitual offender who actually is identified as such, there are four juveniles who would be called 'at risk' of falling into this category. And therein lies the true dilemma of the juvenile justice system.

So what do we learn from this? We learn that we are dealing with people who often come from problem families, people who are very likely to have brothers who will also be in trouble, if they are not already. In looking at the evidence we find that there have been early indications of misconduct and adverse behavior traits; that there has been long-term contact with a number of agencies of the government; that they are likely to become adult career criminals; that they have great potential for violence, including murder; and that they find out that they can manipulate the system early on, because no matter what they do there is nothing that makes an impact on them that they are being treated seriously. We also find that such people recognize that the agencies within the system do not communicate very well with each other. The juvenile justice system is plagued by the bureaucratic tendencies of all governmental agencies, such as inertia, lack of follow-through, depersonalization, fragmentation, inflexibility, and lack of accountability.

The question is simple: how do we translate these lessons gained from what we know about both the casual offender and the serious habitual offender into some recommendations for how the system ought to be improved? The answer to this question can be divided into three parts.

A MORE COMPREHENSIVE APPROACH

First, how do we handle those early contacts, the pre-court contacts and activity in relation to juvenile offenders, whether they be first-time offenders or, more seriously, the habitual offender? The short answer is that one of the things we most need to do is to regroup community services to improve coordination, sharing of information, early intervention and complementary and consistent actions to contain delinquent behavior.

Twenty-five years ago in Oakland, California, there was a serious plague of juvenile problems which caused the City Manager, the Superintendent of Schools, and the Chief of Police to come together and devise just this kind of community services regrouping. They developed in each high school attendance area, of which there were six in the city at that time, a group that was called the Associated Agencies. It brought together on a regular basis the school department, officers from the juvenile division of the police department, probation officers who were dealing with the youth in that area, California Youth Authority parole officers or supervisors in that area, representatives of the Welfare Department, the Health Department, the Housing Department, the Recreation Department, and a coordinator from the City Manager's office. The coordinator provided the authority to ensure participation of all the agencies. But the important thing about it was that they sat in meetings on a regular basis, at least monthly and sometimes weekly, and talked about the troubled families that were in that particular area. What they found as they discussed these cases was that often the Welfare Department might be working with one person, such as a pregnant teenager, while the Police Department might be having trouble with some one else in the family and the School Department was having problems with other children in the family. They also found that in instances where one child was causing problems in high school, there was often another sibling in elementary school on the way up who was going to be a problem in a year or so and had already been identified as having some difficulties either with the police or the schools. As a result, they were able, first of all, to share information so that everybody was knowledgeable about the situation; second, they were able to plan a strategy to deal with the entire family; third, they were able to prevent the juveniles who were already in trouble with the law from playing one agency off against another; and fourth, they were able to try to find solutions that could be followed on a long-term basis.

In order to make this work, there had to be other parts of the structure in place. These groups, you might say, were on the firing line. There was a coordinating committee of middle-management people, the Assistant Superintendent of Schools, and so on, including the County Prosecutor, which met on a quarterly basis to make sure this program was working and to provide policy guidance. The heads of the agencies met on a yearly or semi-yearly basis – the District Attorney himself and the Chief of Police himself – because where the top-level people in the depart-ment were that interested, the people at the lower ranks knew that they had official support and also that somebody was looking over their shoulder to make sure that they were carrying out their responsibilities. The combination of top-level support, coordina-tion, and communication between the agencies, dealing with an entire family, the idea of a definitive action to keep the juvenile from thinking he could beat the system, the follow-up to make sure something got done, the identification of the individual – escaping the anonymity which often is the refuge of the juvenile offenders because they don't think that anybody will know who they are – and the inability to play one agency off against another, all help to change significantly and beneficially the way in which Oakland was able to deal with juvenile crime. It did not solve all the problems, by any means, but it was a major advance that cut down on a great deal of the crime, and in particular it brought together the various agencies to work cooperatively. For example, particular attention was paid at this time to truancy, runaways, and other types of delinquent behavior. Cracking down especially on truancy resulted in decreases in daytime burglaries, as well as other forms of juvenile crime.

This model, of which there are similar examples elsewhere, could be emulated by the appropriate governmental agencies in virtually every area of the United States and United Kingdom. The next step would be to extend this concept by bringing in the social services, including the private agencies, into a closer working relationship with the governmental agencies already mentioned. Such collaboration would provide additional resources to task forces for solving the problems of both individuals and whole families. This would bring the social service agencies into much closer contact with the police, so that police officers would have some options for referral when they see pre-delinquent conduct taking place, but neither have the justification nor deem it appropriate to take the juvenile into custody. One of the most difficult things for a police officer to do when he or she arrives at the scene where juveniles are involved is to decide what to do with the children (knowing that merely turning them over to the parents, if their parents are even available, is not going to be effective in solving the problem). To have these social services brought more closely into the juvenile justice system is a very important part of having a variety of alternatives available.

One additional thing that can be developed around this circle of private social service agencies involves bringing in civic organizations and the business community. The important thing is that there exists a plan, a positive strategy, and an effective coordinating mechanism to make the whole system work more smoothly. Furthermore, that mechanism should begin working even before the first actual crime is committed, when pre-delinquent behavior demonstrates a need for intervention. Ideally, early preventive action can keep the juvenile from ending up in court.

RESPONSIBILITY AND ACCOUNTABILITY IN THE SYSTEM

One of the problems that we have in juvenile court is a need for greater responsibility and accountability, not on the part of the judge, but on the part of those officials who are dealing with the juveniles who come before the court or who become wards of the court. It is important that there be a specific person who has the responsibility for the individual juvenile on a continuing basis. This establishes follow-through continuity and lessens the ability of the juvenile to escape into anonymity. The young offender has to know that someone is watching and that he or she cannot get away with further misconduct. Yet in most probation departments, the agencies that in America carry out the handling of juvenile offenders, you do not find this concept of continuing responsibility and accountability. Far from having an individual who is responsible and who can demand accountability from the offender, one generally finds a whole string of people with whom that juvenile comes into contact. The young person is picked up by the police, often by a patrol officer, perhaps turned over to a juvenile officer, then turned over to an intake officer at the probation department; the case is then turned over to an investigator, and that investigator takes the case and turns it over to the court officer; a different officer may be present at the ultimate disposition in court, who then turns the matter over to a probation officer assigned to supervise the juvenile. If the young person goes to an incarceration facility as part of the disposition, yet another counselor takes over the case. There is no one who actually has responsibility for the juvenile from beginning to end, with whom the youth could relate if he wanted to, or who could develop a long-term rehabilitative program.

One other very important thing that needs to be done in all our courts and juvenile agencies is the sharing of information between organizations. There are sometimes laws that prevent this, but they ought to be changed where they exist. Records must also be accurate and available to document the criminal history of the offender. Furthermore, these records should not be closed when the person is no longer a juvenile and continues to commit felonies. The purpose of having closed records and protecting the identity of juvenile offenders is lost if the juvenile goes on to commit felonies in adulthood. The record of offenses committed prior to age 18 should be available to judges when juvenile delinquents come before criminal courts as adults. Potential offenders should know that this is the way the system works, so that they do not think their past misconduct will be ignored once they become adults. The logic of removing both the stigma of public identification and a past record is clearest for the person who has reformed his conduct and wants to start life as an adult without being haunted by a record of juvenile misdeeds. The person who wants to spend his adult life continuing his criminal career should not have those privileges.

The juvenile court needs more intermediate sanctions than it now has for handling the disposition of the juvenile, so that there are alternatives between merely putting a youthful offender on probation and putting him into some form of what in the United Kingdom is called 'secure accommodation'. Additional options are necessary, including facilities for short stays when the juvenile violates the terms of his probation and needs to be reminded that he owes society and is not merely going to get a slap on the wrist or another line on his record. Violating the terms of his probation, he needs to know that something serious is going to happen, such as a weekend or week in custody. Finally, a critical part of juvenile procedure must be drug testing. Such testing should take place when a person has been arrested as a juvenile and is taken into custody, and at every stage of the proceedings, including during pre-hearing release, while on probation, and during incarceration. Drug abuse occurs in a very high percentage of the juvenile population and one way that accountability can be instilled in juveniles is to let them know that they will be tested regularly and randomly for drug use. The knowledge that they will be tested and held accountable has been found to be one of the best ways to keep people from using drugs again.

PUNISHING CREATIVELY

The third part of the recommendations involves corrections. Community sanctions are a very important alternative to incarceration and, as I mentioned earlier, there must be greater variety available than is presently the case, at least in the United States. But such sanctions must be administered in such a way that they are not viewed by the juvenile as beating the system. In the early 1990s Chief Reuben Greenberg of Charleston, South Carolina, had a very good way to handle this. He brought offenders who were serving time in jail back into the community to remove graffiti and generally clean up. He put them in bright orange jump-suits, which made it clear that they were not there as volunteers in the neighborhood. Perhaps some variation of that could be used when a juvenile is ordered by the court to perform community service. Whatever the disposition is, it must be identified as part of the punishment of the offender so that person cannot come back to the community and pretend that nothing has happened. After all, the people there know that he was arrested and taken away by a police officer. In other words, we have to devise innovative ways to eliminate the idea that the offender has 'beaten the rap'. And, of course, in all community-based sanctions it is important that there be continuing follow-up action and accountability.

Boot camps are another possible sanction. One of the problems that have plagued boot camps in the United States is a fairly negative reaction up until now, largely because some evidence appears to indicate that they do not seem to make much difference in terms of recidivism. One of the reasons this may be so is that the boot camp has not been viewed in the proper light. A boot camp in the military is a fairly harsh, rigidly disciplined period of time. But the armed services do not use it as the *end* of a person's training; rather, they use it as the *beginning*. Perhaps the boot camp idea, which in the juvenile justice context generally involves a six-month period of intense training and discipline, should be followed by a year and a half or so of constructive work activity where youthful offenders are closely supervised at home. Then the expanded boot-camp program would have a combination of experiences beneficial to the individual, much as in the military today, where new recruits visualize boot camp as the beginning of their tour of duty rather than an isolated experience.

There is also the problem that the boot camp itself is too often thought of now as beating the system, however harsh it may be. There was a case in the United States in which a court ruled that boot camps must exist for women, and for girls as well as boys, because the females got the impression that without having boot camps available to them, they could not get out in six months like the males do, and therefore they were serving longer incarcerative sentences. The boot camp is not supposed to be as easy alternative; it is supposed to be a different experience producing rehabilitated individuals. For boot camps to have a beneficial effect, we have to take away the idea that boot camp is somehow a means of getting lenient treatment and avoiding longer incarceration in a jail or prison.

CONCLUSION

Let me suggest, in closing, that there is a need to take a fresh look at the entire juvenile justice system. For example, it might be beneficial for the people who are running correctional institutions, in the adult as well as the juvenile system particularly, to take a new look at what that institution is all about. They should rethink their mission and develop new ideas for achieving their objectives. Too often their perspective is somewhat limited. The counselor or the person in charge of a particular group of inmates for a particular shift is only hoping to get through the night without being knifed or otherwise assaulted. Similarly, the shift supervisor is trying to get through the week without any escapes. The facility superintendent is trying to get through the month without having any correctional officers being arrested for corruption or for bringing in drugs or other contraband; and the director of juvenile facilities is hoping to get through the year without going over his budget. But, in too many cases, nobody is really thinking of the true mission. That mission, at one level, is to provide secure, humane custody; but that must be combined with the responsibility for returning the people they have under their care to constructive citizenship. There has to be a renewal of the mission, which is to make a real effort to return juvenile offenders to society in a state where they will not continue to commit crimes.

One final suggestion as to reform is that we need to broaden our understanding of personnel resources. It has been a tremendous mistake to allow social workers to have a monopoly on juvenile justice positions, even to the extent of requiring advanced degrees in social work for such positions. In order to stretch our resources, one of the things that can be done today is to make use of a resource that is presently abundant: people who are retiring or otherwise leaving the military, who have spent the last 10 to 20 years of their life dealing with young men and women in a constructive way. A number of such people could be brought into the juvenile justice system, perhaps at less expense than those with graduate degrees in social work, but also with much greater life experience and a better chance of performing the rehabilitative activity which has been discussed above.

These are relatively modest recommendations, but they are practical, focused, feasible, and specific. We can talk about the broad concepts for a long time, but if we just take several specific recommendations and start with those we can make considerable progress. If we are to actually improve society's capability to prevent, deter, control, and punish juvenile crime, all parties to the juvenile justice system must take a renewed, reinvigorated, and realistic approach to their responsibilities. Public officials, including legislators, must avoid being mesmerized by the passions or fads of the moment, and must provide instead the policies and resources that will support both long- and short-term initiatives. Police officers, juvenile justice professionals, educators, and other agency participants must rethink their missions, their strategies, their programs, and coordinating mechanisms in order to accomplish the objectives of preventing and controlling juvenile crime. And, indeed, this problem must be made clear to the citizenry, so they will also learn about and support public policies, including adequate funding and adequate personnel to serve the needs of dependent and delinquent youth while protecting the public against juvenile crime. All of these groups need to look toward realism and progress in improving our juvenile justice system so that it is both effective and just.

6 Law, Morality and the Common Good

Jonathan Sacks

The Hebrew Bible paints a strange picture of the people of the covenant. The Israelites emerge from its pages as a stiff-necked and backsliding people, often lapsing into idolatry and dissent. A detached reader of the Bible must find himself asking: why did God choose this people from among all others to be His special witnesses? The book of Genesis answers this question at only one point, and the answer is striking. Genesis 18: 19 tells us that God said of Abraham: 'I have chosen him so that he will instruct his children and his household after him to keep the way of the Lord by doing what is right [*tzedek*] and just [*mishpat*].' *Tzedek* and *mishpat* are both legal virtues. We might best translate them, respectively, as distributive and procedural justice.

The verse suggests that whatever else Abraham's children might do or not do, they would respect the ideals of justice and the rule of law. This, the Bible implies, is a transcending virtue, one that may compensate for many shortcomings. And this is surely a cardinal feature of the Hebrew Bible and of the Jewish contribution to civilization ever since: the belief that a people, a nation and a society are judged by the extent to which justice and the rule of law prevail. Few religions have placed law and its just administration so close to the heart of its concerns.

Throughout the Pentateuch we find repeated injunctions to this end. 'Judges and officers shalt thou make thee in all thy gates ... and they shall judge the people with righteous judgement ... Justice, justice shalt thou pursue that thou mayest live' (Deuteronomy 16: 18–20). Moses, in appointing judges, tells them to 'Hear the causes between your brethren, and judge righteously between a man and his brother, and the stranger that is with him. You shall not respect persons in judgement. You shall

99

hear the small and the great alike. You shall not be afraid of the face of any man, for judgement belongs to God' (Deuteronomy 1: 16–17).

At the core of the covenant is a magnificent legal code which reaches its most exalted expression in the Ten Commandments communicated by God Himself to the assembled Israelites at Mount Sinai. In the prophetic books the rule of law becomes a momentous and moving vision: 'Let justice roll down like a river, and righteousness as a never-ending stream' (Amos 5: 24).

Never has this idea lost its power or relevance. For such seems to be the unalterable or at least not yet altered constitution of human nature – that we are prone to conflict. And unless regulated by law, conflict finds its resolution in violence, war, tyranny, inequity, the defence of privilege, the oppression of the powerless, and the substitution of might – economic, political or military – for right. Against all these, the Hebrew Bible offers the alternative of law, a law that treats great and small alike, that owes its ultimate authority to a power beyond all earthly rulers, a law that bears the signature of transcendence.

Although this noble proposition has since become the shared property of human civilisation, Paul Johnson rightly reminds us of its origin:

Certainly the world without the Jews would have been a radically different place. Humanity might eventually have stumbled upon all the Jewish insights. But we cannot be sure. All the great conceptual discoveries of the intellect seem obvious and inescapable once they have been revealed, but it requires a special genius to formulate them for the first time. The Jews had this gift. To them we owe the idea of equality before the law, both divine and human; of the sanctity of life and the dignity of the human person; of the individual conscience and so of personal redemption; of the collective conscience and so of social responsibility; of peace as an abstract ideal and love as the foundation of justice, and many other items which constitute the basic moral furniture of the human mind. Without the Jews it might have been a much emptier place.

THE MINIMALIST CONCEPTION OF LAW

Having paid this tribute to law and the Hebrew Bible and the relationship between them, I want to focus on a subject which has been the cause of much debate, not only in our time, but at many other critical junctures in civilisation. I refer to the *scope* of law and its role in society, to law's place in the ultimate scheme of things.

I want to contrast two conceptions of law, one exemplified by the Jewish tradition, the other known to it and indeed accepted by it, but not as an ideal. I call them, respectively, the *maximalist* and *minimalist* interpretations, and these terms will become clearer as we proceed. Doubtless, no actual legal system conforms to either of these two idealized types, but I present them as contrasts for the sake of clarity. I begin with the system Jews did *not* adopt for themselves, although they recognized its validity and at times its necessity, namely the minimalist conception of law.

My starting point is the Mishnaic tractate of *Avot*, known as the 'Ethics of the Fathers', an anthology compiled in the first half of the third century of the Common Era, though its component texts have an earlier origin. The rabbis quoted in *Avot* took a sceptical view of public life. 'Be careful in your dealings with the ruling powers', said the sages, 'for they only befriend a man when it serves their purposes, but they do not stand by him in his hour of need' (*Avot* 2: 5). None the less they recognized the need for government and the rule of law, and they did so in the form of a famous statement. 'Rabbi Hanina the deputy High Priest used to say: Pray for the welfare of the government, for were it not that people stood in fear of it, they would swallow one another alive' (*Avot* 3: 2).

On the face of it this is an early anticipation of Thomas Hobbes' description of society in a state of nature: a war of all against all in which life would be, in his phrase, 'nasty, brutish and short'. However, a close examination of the text reveals a peculiar poignancy to Rabbi Hanina's remarks. A manuscript reading of the Mishnah yields a text in which Rabbi Hanina's statement appears not in the third but in the first person: not 'they' but '*we* would have swallowed up each other alive'.

To understand the significance of this detail we must recall Rabbi Hanina's formal office, that of deputy High Priest. This allows us to date his remark with some precision. Rabbi Hanina lived during the last days of the second Temple, in the second half of the first century CE. He officiated there. He was a senior member of the priesthood. We can now sense the full pathos of his dictum.

Rabbi Hanina lived through the destruction of the second Temple by the Romans, one of the greatest catastrophes to have befallen the Jewish people. It led to nearly nineteen centuries of dispersion, powerlessness and persecution. We know from Josephus, however, that while the Romans were at the gates, within the walls of the beseiged Jerusalem a divided Jewish people was engaged in bitter and self-destructive civil war.

The government of which Rabbi Hanina spoke was not a Jewish government but none other than the Roman power which had desecrated Judaism's Holy of Holies and destroyed its central religious institutions. None the less, he prayed for its welfare and urged others to do so. For he had seen, within Jerusalem beseiged, the terrifying spectacle of life without law, the war of all against all. Any law is better than no law. Hence the minimalist definition of law as the instrument which prevents us from swallowing each other alive, or as John Stuart Mill was to put it eighteen centuries later: 'The only purpose for which power can rightfully be exercised over any member of a civilised community against his will is to prevent harm to others.'

Mill arrived at this conclusion in a book entitled *On Liberty*. He believed that the cause of liberty was best served by having as little law as possible, or at least by marking out certain territories as being – as the Wolfenden Committee on Homosexuality put it – 'crudely and simply not the law's business'. But this is not the only or even the most helpful way of reaching the conclusion. Jews, for example, have always cherished liberty since the exodus from slavery in Egypt. None the less, for Judaism freedom is not achieved by restricting the scope of law. It is precisely a life lived *within* the law, a law that covers all aspects of life.

A more helpful way of understanding the minimalist conception is that it arises in a society in which the concept of a common good, promulgated by the central institutions and educational structures of its culture, has eroded or is beginning to erode. We have seen one way in which this can happen. There were few values held in common by the deputy High Priest Hanina and the Roman government which had destroyed his people's Temple. There is another way in which it can happen. A society can move to a less collective, more individualistic sense of morality. Such was beginning to be the case in 1859 when Mill wrote his treatise on liberty, and the process has continued unabated to this day.

Under either circumstance, an extensive system of laws can come to seem an unwarrantable intrusion into the lives of individuals, minority groups or subject populations. Law is necessary, but it should be kept to a minimum, defined as the prevention of harm to others. It is an infringement on liberty. Therefore, though there must be law, there should be as little as possible, at any rate in matters where we regard liberty as of the essence, especially those involving moral judgement.

A MAXIMALIST CONCEPTION OF LAW

Against this I want to contrast the Judaic view of Jewish law, one that I will call a maximalist conception. I refer here to a set of beliefs with a long and continuous history, originating in the Pentateuch, echoed in other books of the Bible and given consistent expression in the rabbinic literature from the first centuries of the Common Era to today.

This view can be characterized in three propositions. The first is this. Not only does the religion of the Hebrew Bible contain laws which carry the legislative authority of God himself, but it is *through law* that God chooses to reveal Himself to mankind. When God speaks to the assembled Israelites at Mount Sinai and to Moses at other times, what He communicates is not oracles about the future nor metaphysical truths about the nature of reality but *Torah*, law, and *mitzvot*, commandments.

To be sure, God in the Hebrew Bible is a God of miracles, redemption and grace. He intervenes in history, rescues His people and offers them – if they will live by His law – protection and prosperity. But this is, as it were, secondary to the essence of the covenant, about which Moses reminds the people in these words:

> See, I have taught you decrees and laws as the Lord my God commanded me, so that you may follow them in the land you are entering ... Observe them carefully, for this will show your wisdom and understanding to the nations who will hear about all these decrees and say, 'Surely this great nation is a wise and understanding people' ... What other nation is so great as to have such righteous decrees and laws as this body of laws I am setting before you this day? (Deuteronomy 4: 5–8).

Psalm 199 presents this same proposition from the perspective of personal spirituality:

> I will always obey your law, for ever and ever. I will walk about in freedom, for I have sought out Your precepts. I will speak of Your statutes before kings and will not be put to shame, for I delight in your commandments because I love them (Psalm 119: 44–7).

Two striking expressions of this view are to be found in statements of the early rabbinic sages in the Babylonian and Jerusalem Talmuds. One declares: 'From the day the Temple was destroyed, the Holy One, blessed be he, has nothing in this world except the four cubits of law.' The other attributes to God the statement: 'Would that My children forsake Me and yet occupy themselves in the study of My law, for the light it contains would bring them back to Me.' In short: *if we seek God we will find Him in law*. Admittedly, God reveals himself in nature and history as well. But neither nature nor history point as unambiguously to the existence of God as does law.

The second proposition, and perhaps the single greatest contribution of Israel to the religious heritage of mankind, is what is often called ethical monotheism: the idea that God is not merely the author of the moral law but is Himself bound by it. It is this that gives rise to some of the most awe-inspiring passages in the Bible in which Moses, Jeremiah, Job and others argue with God on the basis of the shared code of justice and mercy which binds both creature and Creator, reaching a climax in the question of Abraham: 'Shall the Judge of all the earth not do justice?'

For Judaism, the connection between religion, law and morality is this. God and man come together to form a covenant which binds both to a morality which each recognizes as righteous and just, much as two partners come together to form a marriage which both recognize as imposing obligations. Neither God nor man arbitrarily invent morality, just as neither husband nor wife invent marriage. By entering into a covenant, both agree to bind themselves to one another within its terms. Thus love is translated into a moral relationship whose terms are law.

So there is a substantive relationship between God and law, and between law and morality. Admittedly, it is loose rather than precise. There is much law in the Bible whose content we could call ritual, not moral. And there is much morality in the Bible – such as Leviticus' command to love one's neighbour as oneself – which is not articulated in the form of a detailed code of law. But the connection is of the essence of religious life.

The picture set forth in the Bible is not one of *legal positivism*, in which, to quote Austin, 'The existence of the law is one thing; its merit or demerit is another.' Nor is it one of *natural law*, in which obligation flows from human nature. Law, as portrayed in the Bible, is *covenantal*. It is born in the mutual agreement of God and humanity to engage in constructing a society on the foundations of compassion, righteousness and justice.

The third and most distinctive feature of Judaism is the connection between law and *education*. It can best be expressed in the proposition that Judaism expects its adherents not merely to obey the law, but to be lawyers: *students* of the law. Indeed, this is one of the meanings of the phrase in which God, in giving the Ten Commandments to Israel, calls on them to become a 'kingdom of priests'. For the priest in biblical times was not only one who served in the Temple but also one who acted as a judge and instructed the people in the law.

In a biblical passage which Jews recite several times daily, we are told: 'You shall teach these [laws] diligently to your children, speaking of them when you sit at home and when you travel on a journey, when you lie down and when you rise up.' On the brink of exodus from Egypt, Moses instructs the Israelites not merely in a variety of laws, but also in how to teach and explain these laws to their children in generations to come. From the days of Ezra, if not before, the heroes of Israel have been its teachers. And by the first century of the Common Era, Jews had established the first system of free, compulsory and universal education known to history – an education first and foremost in the law.

The question is why. Here we can only speculate, but the reason seems straightforward. Inescapably there is a conflict between the rule of law and individual freedom. A civilization can resolve this conflict in a variety of ways. It can place a low value on the rule of law, and thus favour anarchy. It can place a low value on individual liberty, and thus favour tyranny. It can make a third choice, the one favoured by John Stuart Mill, H. L. A. Hart, Ronald Dworkin and other liberal thinkers, which is to say that liberty is a supreme if not always overriding value, and that therefore the domain of law should be restricted in areas where personal choice is particularly important. As Dworkin puts it in his recent book, *Life's Dominion*: 'Whatever view we take about abortion and euthanasia, we want the right to decide for ourselves, and we should therefore be ready to insist that any honourable constitution, any genuine constitution of principle, will guarantee that right for everyone.'

Dworkin presents this as a conclusion to which any reasonable individual would be forced. But in one respect I believe he is wrong. The Hebrew Bible places a high, even a supreme, value on the individual and on freedom. The individual is, as the first chapter of Genesis states, made in the image of God. As the Mishnah puts it: 'One who saves a single life is as if he saved an entire universe.' Freedom, too, is of the essence of serving God. Israel's history begins with an act of liberation, and the laws of the Sabbath, the Sabbatical and Jubilee years and the many laws providing aid to the poor are all practical expressions of a social order designed to minimise the varieties of enslavement. So the Bible sets a high value on the individual and on freedom, but *it sets an equally high value on law*. How then does it reconcile the apparent conflict between these principles?

The answer lies in a particular concept of education, one sharply at odds with prevailing moral fashion but which can be found in Aristotle and until relatively recently might even have been described as self-evident. On this view education is not simply a matter of imparting information, inculcating skills and training the individual to make autonomous choices. Instead, it is a matter of *inducting successive generations into the society in which they will become participants*. It involves transmitting a particular society's history, norms and 'habits of the heart'. Education is an *apprenticeship in being a citizen*. It is a process of learning certain rules and then internalizing them so that the law is no longer an external constraint but becomes, in Jeremiah's phrase, a law 'written in our inmost being and inscribed upon our hearts' (Jeremiah 31: 33). Law then represents not a set of regulations but that configuration of character that the Aristotelian and Maimonidean traditions call virtue.

The Judaic connection between law and education is this: that only when our sensibilities are educated by the law can we associate the law with freedom rather than with constraint, and say with the Psalmist, 'I will walk about in freedom, for I have sought out Your precepts.' Teaching, instruction or education – understood as the transmission of a moral tradition across the generations – resolves the conflict between liberty and law without forcing us to choose between anarchy and tyranny. Law is seen as part of a moral order which, to the extent that it is internalized as self-restraint, does not need to be enforced by external agencies such as police, courts and punishment. Education becomes the guardian of liberty, because it maximizes the degree to which civil society is sustained by self-imposed restraints and minimizes the degree to which we depend on the intervention of outside force. The more law is inscribed upon our hearts, the less it needs to be policed in the streets.

This, then, is the portrait of law we find in the Bible. To this I add one final observation. For there is an obvious question to be raised. Why does the Hebrew Bible emphasize law more than (though it does not neglect) individual salvation and private faith? Surely law is a highly secular phenomenon. It deals in matters of this world, the original meaning of the Latin *saecularis*.

Religion, surely, is a private transaction within the soul and bears only tangentially on legislation, crime, punishment and the social order?

The answer, I believe, is this. The Hebrew Bible portrays God as One concerned above all with how we behave towards others. God is to be found in relationships, and relationships take place within the framework of society and its institutions and rules. Faith is thus linked with morality, and morality is an essentially shared, collaborative endeavour. Its smallest unit is the family, its largest unit is humanity, and between them lies a variety of communities from the neighbourhood to the nation state. What morality is not and cannot be is a private enterprise, a form of self-expression. What liberal individualism takes as the highest virtue – each person doing that which is right in his own eyes – is for the Bible (Deuteronomy 12: 8, Judges 17: 6; 21: 25) the absence or abdication of virtue, and indeed a way of describing the disintegration of society.

MORALITY AND LAW

This takes us directly to the present. In 1959, Lord Devlin delivered a lecture which subsequently became the basis of much discussion, entitled 'Morals and the Criminal Law'. In it he said this:

> Societies disintegrate from within more frequently than they are broken up by external pressures. There is disintegration when no common morality is observed and history shows that the loosening of moral bonds is often the first stage of disintegration, so that society is justified in taking the same steps to preserve its moral code as it does to preserve its government and other essential institutions.

That argument was rejected, and since then many laws thought to have a moral or religious basis have been repealed or liberalized. But something else has happened, almost without comment. What provoked Lord Devlin's response was a sentence in the report of the Wolfenden Committee (1957) which said this: 'Unless a deliberate attempt is to be made by society, acting through the agency of the law, to equate the sphere of crime with that of sin, there must remain a realm of private morality and immorality which is, in brief and crude terms, not the law's business.' The report then added, by way of postscript, 'To say this is not to condone or encourage private immorality.'

Let me say, lest I be misunderstood, that on the substantive point I agree with Wolfenden. Jewish law itself draws a clear distinction between matters to be adjudicated by a human court and those where judgement is the exclusive prerogative of God. However, subsequent experience has shown one thing to be false, namely the assumption that you can change the law while leaving morality untouched. The authors of the Report evidently believed that homosexuality could cease to be a crime while remaining a sin in the public mind. It would no longer be punished; it would merely be denounced. Morality would not be enforced by law. It would instead be reinforced by teaching and preaching.

That attractive prospect has proved to be unfounded. The extent to which changes in the law set in motion a wholly unforeseen series of developments can best be measured by this fact: that were the authors of the Wolfenden Report to repeat today that certain sexual behaviours whilst not criminal are nonetheless sinful, they would find themselves banned from most British classrooms and American universities on the grounds of 'homophobia'. The liberalization of the law has led to an astonishingly rapid eclipse of the very idea that there are shared moral norms. What a single generation ago was the avant garde of radical liberalism would today be seen as the politically incorrect face of moral fundamentalism.

We are all too familiar with the consequences. An environment in which moral judgement is condemned as being judgemental, in which the one concept to have universal currency is that of rights but in which there are no agreed criteria by which to adjudicate between conflicting rights, in which the idea has become an orthodoxy that there is no sexual ethic beyond the consistent application of personal choice, has caused the disintegration of one after another of the bases of our shared moral universe. In such an environment there can be no moral authority beyond the self or the sect of the like-minded. There can be no moral institutions, such as that of the family, in which obligations self-evidently override personal preference. There can be no moral role-models who epitomize our collective values and virtues, because we are too divided to reach a consensus on whether to prefer Mother Teresa to Madonna. There can, in short, be nothing beyond the random aggregation of individuals and groups living in accidental proximity, each with its own lifestyle, each claiming our attention for the duration of a sound-bite. The moral voice has been replaced by noise, coherence by confusion, and society itself by a series of discreet particles called individuals.

It is as if, in the 1950s and 1960s, without intending to, we had set a time-bomb ticking which would eventually explode the moral framework into fragments. The human cost has been colossal, most visibly in terms of marriage and the family. There has been a proliferation of one-parent families, deserted wives and neglected and abused children. But the cost has been far wider in terms of the loss of authority, institutions in crisis, and what Durkheim called *anomie*, the loss of a public sense of moral order.

It is precisely at such times that an immense burden is placed upon the law, law specifically in the minimalist sense I described above. Law at such points in the history of civilization is seen not as the expression of something wider and deeper, what Leslie Stephen described as 'the seal on the wax of moral sentiment'. Rather it is seen as an external constraint, limited to the prevention of harm to others. But because our internal constraints have been eroded, the police, the courts and Parliament are hard pressed to contain the tide of crime. And because we no longer have a shared moral code, the law is called on to decide what has become effectively undecidable, namely what *constitutes* harm to others. Does abortion? Does the withdrawal of a life-support machine? Does the destruction of an embryo created by *in vitro* fertilization?

We turn to the law to answer such questions for us, as Americans have recently turned to the law to tell them what constitutes sexual harassment or adequate fatherhood. But the law no longer reflects moral consensus because there is no consensus for it to reflect. The law is placed in an increasingly invidious situation as we expect more from it and as society's moral code and institutions give it less and less support. The law becomes our only authority in an age which is hostile to authority as such. The result is the situation described in the opening words of the book of Ruth, conventionally translated as 'In the days when the judges judged', but which rabbinic tradition translated as 'In the days when society judged its judges'.

We are, I believe, at a difficult time for religion, morality and the law. There is only a fine line dividing liberalism from individualism, and freedom from the disintegration of the concept of the common good. My own view is this. Though I value the contribution of liberalism to the opening up of society to a multitude of voices, we are in danger of finding ourselves having gone too far in abandoning the idea of society as a shared moral project, and this will have tragic consequences for both our public and our private lives. There are things we cannot achieve without collaborative effort framed by shared rules, roles and virtues. Among them are peace, compassion, justice, and the resolution of conflict in a way that both sides can see as fair. These are the very things by which, according to the Hebrew Bible, God judges that most risky of His undertakings: the creation of mankind.

We cannot undo what we have done. Having de-legislated large sectors of morality we cannot re-legislate them. The necessary consent has gone and there is no point in moral nostalgia, fondly remembering the days when you could go out leaving your front door unlocked. But we can summon the courage to rebuild a moral consensus, beginning with that most fundamental of questions: what sort of world would we wish to bequeath to our children and grandchildren?

I believe that the law needs and deserves this from all who have moral influence in our society, not least from religious leaders. We must have the courage to make judgements, to commend some ways of life and point to the shortcomings of others, however much this offends against the canons of our non-judgemental culture. We must lead by moral vision and example, and be prepared to challenge the icons of individualism, the idolatry of our age.

My argument, then, is this. At a certain point in the history of civilizations, a moral consensus breaks down. The connection between law and morality becomes problematic, and an attempt is made to solve the problem by conceiving law in minimalist terms. It is there to do no more than to prevent harm to others, to prevent us, in Rabbi Hanina's words, from swallowing one another alive. The passage of time, however, invariably exposes the contradiction at the heart of this idea. Law is left to solve problems which it cannot solve alone. We then painfully rediscover the ancient truth of the Hebrew Bible, that the rule of law is compatible with a sense of personal liberty only when supported by at least some collective moral code and by an educational system which allows successive generations to internalize it. Society cannot live by law alone. It needs our common commitment to the common good.

Part III
Teaching Virtue in Juvenile Justice, Family and Educational Settings

7 Juvenile Probation on the Eve of the Next Millennium

Ronald P. Corbett, Jr.

INTRODUCTION

Judge Judith Sheindlin, supervising judge for the Manhattan Family Court, published in 1996 her perspective on the state of affairs in juvenile justice in a book titled, *Don't Pee on My Leg and Tell Me It's Raining*. Judge Sheindlin's views, graphically foreshadowed in the title, include a repudiation of the social causation approach to juvenile delinquency and a call for a return to an ethic of self-discipline and individual accountability. From the vantage-point of over 20 years' experience as a juvenile judge, Sheindlin sees a system that can 'barely function', trading in empty threats and broken promises (p. 5). Juvenile courts, in her view, have avoided assigning blame for wrongdoing and have thereby encouraged a lack of individual responsibility, leaving young offenders with ready excuses for their predatory behavior and completely without fear of any consequences. The system must 'cut through the baloney and tell the truth', starting with the 'total elimination of probation' in favor of a greater reliance on police surveillance and increased incarceration (p. 61).

While more extreme than most, Sheindlin's damning critique of the juvenile justice system is of a piece with a number of recent treatments of the system, both journalistic and academic. A brief synopsis of each suggests a system in a severe state of crisis.

In *No Matter How Loud I Shout*, Edward Humes (1996), a Pulitzer-Prize-winning author, presents an inside view of the workings of the Los Angeles Juvenile Court. Describing the system generally as 'broken, battered and outgunned' (p. 371), Humes echoes Sheindlin's theme of a widespread sense of immunity among juvenile offenders, perpetuated by a system that dispenses wrist slaps and apple bites in lieu of real sanctions. Facing continuous delays instead of prompt justice and infrequent phone contact from probation officers instead of the close supervision needed, the young offenders in Los Angeles quickly learn that they are beyond the reach of the law:

> That's how the system programs you. They let you go and they know that just encourages you, and then they can get you on something worse later on. It's like, they set you up. Of course, I'm to blame, too, for going along with it. I didn't have to do those things, I know that. But the system didn't have to make it so goddamn easy. (Humes, 1996, p. 333)

In *The State of Violent Crime in America*, the first report of the newly formed Council on Crime in America (1996), the juvenile system is portrayed as a revolving door where, again, the theme of the lack of consequences and the consequent emboldening of young offenders is struck. Chaired by former Attorney General Griffin Bell and well-known conservative intellectual William Bennett, the report illustrates the success of one jurisdiction (Jacksonville, Florida) with the increased use of adult punishments for serious juvenile offenders, and generally calls for a sober realization that the juvenile justice system's traditional reliance on treatment interventions must give way to strategies based on incapacitation and punishment.

Finally, in *Screwing the System and Making It Work*, an ethnographic study of an unnamed juvenile court system, sociologist Mark Jacobs (1990) depicts a system whose principle intervention – community supervision – is demonstrably failing, and whose state of disorganization and administrative weakness undermines any attempt at effective solutions. The few successes that Jacobs finds are accomplished in spite of the system by creatively evading the rules and regulations which otherwise frustrate all reasonable efforts. In the end, Jacobs concludes that the juvenile justice system fails because it attempts to solve problems of social breakdown through the largely ineffectual means of individual treatment plans.

Even granting that exposés will always earn publication more quickly than positive coverage, these four notable publications have such convergent findings that a conclusion regarding a crisis state in juvenile justice generally, and juvenile probation specifically, seems inescapable. What then should be done? What initiatives might be undertaken in probation that would set juvenile justice on a more promising course, earning it back a measure of public trust and genuine impact on the lives of young offenders? This article will attempt to answer those questions by first reviewing the scope of the work of juvenile probation and current trends in juvenile crime, then reviewing what has been learned about successful correctional interventions and how those lessons can be applied to juvenile probation, concluding with an examination of a new model for juvenile justice that can incorporate the findings of research in a context that values the rights and expectations of offenders, victims and society.

JUVENILE PROBATION IN THE UNITED STATES

In a nationwide review of juvenile probation published in 1996 by the Office of Juvenile Justice and Delinquency Prevention, Torbet reports an annual caseflow of nearly 1.5 million delinquency cases, resulting in some 500 000 juveniles under probation at any given time. In the United States, juvenile probation officers have caseloads averaging 41 offenders, although much higher averages are commonly found in urban areas.

Duties of juvenile probation officers are multiple but chiefly fall into the following three categories: intake, screening and assessment; pre-sentence investigations; and supervision.

Juvenile probation officers in many jurisdictions are charged with the responsibility of determining whether arrested juveniles will proceed to a formal court process or instead be diverted to a informal process, if the offense involved is minor. In making this recommendation, the officer will obtain from the offender, his/her family and any social agencies involved with the juvenile at least a threshold amount of current status and background information, including school attendance, behavior at home and in the community, family relationships, peers, etc. A great deal of emphasis in screening will be placed on the circumstances of the offense and previous record, if any. In addition to recommending for or against diversion, this intake process will yield pertinent information for the juvenile judge to utilize in making decisions regarding detention, bail, conditions of release, appointment of counsel and other matters.

Probation officers play a crucial role in determining the most appropriate sentence or disposition to be imposed on the juvenile before the court. In preparing such reports, probation officers will begin by expanding information gathered at intake as well as reaching out to other officials, treatment personnel and family that may have useful information or perspectives bearing on the issue of an appropriate disposition. Pre-sentence reports will typically include as major sections a detailed examination of the facts and circumstances surrounding the offense and the juvenile's role in the incident; an elaborate social history, including any professional evaluations undertaken at the request of the court or the family; a summary of the impact of the delinquency on the victim(s) and their views regarding an appropriate disposition; and a discussion of the elements of an ideal disposition, including the alternatives available along with the probation officer's recommendation (National Center for Juvenile Justice, 1991).

The bulk of the work of juvenile probation officers is consumed in supervising youth placed by the courts on probation. This supervision includes both direct and regular contact with the offender (where resources permit), as well as collateral work with parents, schools, employers, and agency personnel. It is the probation officer's responsibility to enforce the orders of the court in the form of victim restitution or curfews, to oversee the activities of the offender as much as possible, to uncover any lapses in behavior or company, and to insure that the juvenile takes advantage of all opportunities for addressing personal problems, such as substance abuse or school failings. While the ideal is to insure full compliance with all the conditions of probation and to see that the juvenile leaves probation better equipped for a law-abiding life than when supervision began, probation officers must also respond quickly to non-compliance, and must move for revocation of probation and a more serious sentence when circumstances warrant it. In discharging this core function of supervision, effective probation must play many roles – police officer, counselor, family therapist, educator, mentor, and disciplinarian. It is the successful juggling of these multiple roles, assessing which is most appropriate in a given situation, that leads to the most effective practice.

Recent Trends

Trends within the juvenile probation system are ominous. The number of delinquency petitions increased by 23 per cent between 1989 and 1993, leading to a 21 per cent increase in probation caseloads. At the same time, there has been no concomitant increase in resources provided to the juvenile courts, although the public demand for accountability and hard-nosed, intensive treatment of juveniles before the courts has become most pronounced (Torbet, 1996).

More worrisome still is the worsening profile of the juveniles coming before the courts. Even though most youth placed on probation are adjudicated for property offenses, the percentage placed on probation for violent offenses has increased significantly in the last years. In 1989, 17 per cent of those youth on probation were adjudicated for violent offenses; by 1993 that percentage had increased to 21 per cent, which translates into a 24 per cent growth in the proportion of violent offenders on juvenile probation (Torbet, 1996).

This trend has changed the character of probation work for many juvenile officers, who now must reckon with safety issues of a new dimension. A recent Justice Department survey found that one-third of probation officers polled had been assaulted in the line of duty and that 42 per cent reported themselves as being either usually or always concerned for their safety (Torbet, 1996).

This problem is amplified by the widely held view that today's juveniles have a degree of unprecedented cold-bloodedness and remorselessness. While difficult to quantify in terms of traditional research, it has been this author's experience that within both probation and police circles, discussion has been pervaded by the theme of a growing and alarming lack of concern and emotion among young offenders for the consequences to their victims, or even themselves, of their involvement in serious violence. This is the new face of juvenile crime, and it is a major departure from past experience, leaving few reliable blueprints for action available to concerned officials. In this connection James Q. Wilson, a professor of public policy at the University of California-Los Angeles, has referred to 'youngsters who afterwards show us the blank, unremorseful stare of a feral, presocial being' (quoted in DiIulio, 1996).

The Coming Plague of Juvenile Violence

In a *New York Times* column in the summer of 1996, Princeton criminologist John DiIulio described the juvenile violence problems as 'grave and growing'. The following trends underline DiIulio's concern and provide further evidence of an explosion of juvenile violence that has the potential to overwhelm America's big cities. While most trends in adult arrests for violent crime are down since 1990, juvenile arrests for serious violence increased 26 per cent by 1994, including a 15 per cent increase in murder. Furthermore, the number of juveniles murdered grew by 82 per cent between 1984 and 1994. Finally, the juvenile arrest rates for weapons violations nearly doubled between 1987 and 1994; similarly, while in 1980 the number of juveniles murdered by firearm was 47 per cent, by 1994 that figure had grown to 67 per cent (Snyder *et al.*, 1996).

Researchers have been able to attribute the greatest part of the increase in juvenile homicides to firearm-related murders. Blumstein (1996) has offered an analysis of this increase that traces its origins to the emergence of the crack cocaine trade in the mid-1980s and the acquisition of firearms that was a unique aspect of that emerging criminal enterprise. Young people who obtained guns originally for business purposes would also have them available in the event of other, more conventional types of conflicts among youth. The wider circulation and possession of firearms by the 'players' caused other youth not involved in the drug trade to pick up guns for self-protection, as they did not wish to leave themselves at a tactical disadvantage.

Related research confirms that although firearm-related deaths among youth may be commonly seen as related to the drug trade, in fact most such homicides are a by-product of a violent argument rather than an event occurring during the commission of a crime. It becomes plain, then, that strategies to reduce the most serious juvenile crime must address the issue of reducing gun possessions, an issue to be taken up later in this discussion.

Two additional observations help frame the future of juvenile violence. It is commonly accepted that rates of juvenile crime, including violence, are driven by a demographic imperative. That is, as the number of people in the crime-prone age bracket – the teens and early twenties – ebbs and flows, so generally does the crime rate (Fox, 1996). The bad news in this respect is that America is entering a 10- to 15-year span when the crime-prone age cohort will increase substantially. For example, by the year 2000 there will be a million more people between the ages of 14 and 17 than there were in 1995, of which roughly half will be male (Wilson, 1995a). By the year 2010 there will be 74 million juveniles under the age of 17 (DiIulio, 1996). These estimates have left DiIulio and others to project that juvenile participation in murder, rape, and robbery will more than double by 2010.

However, the most recent data, while limited, is promising. During 1995, for the first time in 10 years, the rate of juvenile homicide decreased for the second year in a row, by 15.2 per cent (Butterfield, 1996). In a report issued by the US Department of Justice, data gathered by the FBI revealed that the juvenile homicide rate, which reached an all-time high in 1993, declined over the following two years by 22.8 per cent. While a two-year trend is certainly encouraging, it is too soon to predict that the demographic forces are inoperative. Murders by young people are still alarmingly high and, as the number of teenagers increases over the next several years, it will take hard work and good fortune to sustain the currently hopeful trend.

LESSONS LEARNED ABOUT EFFECTIVE INTERVENTIONS

While one could hardly guess it from the current tone of relentless punitiveness pervading the debates on criminal justice policy, there has been a near-exponential increase over the last 15 years in solid research about the characteristics of effective correctional interventions. While the amount of public funds devoted to criminal research pales in comparison with that devoted to other forms of basic research (such as health issues), researchers have none the less made important advances in our understanding of the ingredients necessary to end criminal and delinquent careers (Petersilia, 1991).

Canadian criminologists Don Andrews and Paul Gendreau have been at the leading edge of this research. By employing the relatively new statistical technique of meta-analysis, which allows for combining the results of multiple studies of a similar type to test the aggregate strength of a given intervention, Andrews and Gendreau (1990) have been able to identify key factors that can be utilized in the construction of correctional programs, factors which when used in combination can reduce recidivism by as much as 50 per cent. Their research looked equally at juvenile and adult programs and found commonalities across the two groups. In summary, effective programs had the following common features:

1. They are intensive and behavioral. Intensity was measured by both the absorption of the offender's daily schedule and the duration of the program over time. Appropriate services in this respect will occupy 40 to 70 per cent of the offender's time and last an average of 6 months. Behavioral programs will establish a regimen of positive reinforcements for pro-social behavior and will incorporate a modeling approach, including demonstrations of positive behavior that offenders are then encouraged to imitate;
2. They target high-risk offenders and criminogenic needs. Somewhat surprisingly, effective programs worked best with offenders classified as high-risk. This effect is strengthened if the program first identifies the presence of individual needs known to predict recidivism (e.g., substance abuse, poor self-control) and then focuses on eliminating the problem;
3. Treatment modalities and counselors must be matched with individual offender types, a principle Andrews and Gendreau

refer to as 'responsivity'. The program approach much be matched with the learning style and personality of the offender – a one-size-fits-all approach will fail. Taking care to compare the style of any therapist/counselor with the personality of the offender (anxious offenders, for example, should be matched with especially sensitive counselors) is also critical;
4. They provide pro-social contexts and activities and emphasize advocacy and brokerage. Effective programs will replace the normal offender networks with new circles of peers and contacts who are involved in law-abiding lifestyles. Success will be enhanced by aggressive efforts to link offenders with community agencies offering needed services. Most offenders will be unfamiliar with strategies for working in the community and effective programs can serve as a bridge to facilitate a kind of mainstreaming of offenders. (Gendreau, 1996)

Lipsey (1995) undertook a meta-analysis of some 400 juvenile programs and reached conclusions similar to those of Andrews and Gendreau (1990). Lipsey's findings are impressive due to the much greater number of programs included in his analysis and the fact that he restricted his study to juvenile programs. In addition to those findings that parallel earlier results, Lipsey further discovered that skill-building programs and those that were closely monitored for program implementation and integrity, usually by a research team, were successful.

EFFECTIVENESS OF SPECIFIC PROGRAMS

Traditional Probation

Despite the fact that it is clearly the treatment of choice for most juvenile offenders, there has been amazingly little major research on the effectiveness of regular probation. Although targeted at only a small percentage of the overall probation population, researchers' monies and efforts have commonly been devoted to more recent innovations such as intensive supervision, electronic monitoring, or boot camps.

One noteworthy exception to this trend is a study published in 1988 by Wooldredge, in which he analyzed the impact of four different types of dispositions – including traditional probation – imposed by Illinois juvenile courts. This study of the subsequent recidivism of over 2000 delinquents found that lengthy probation supervision, if combined with community treatment, had the greatest effect in suppressing later recidivism, particularly when compared with incarceration or outright dismissal. Wooldredge concludes as follows:

> While it appears that 'doing something' is [usually] better than 'doing nothing' for eliminating recidivism, this study suggests that differences in 'something' may also yield differences in recidivism rates. Specifically, two years of court supervision with community treatment is superior to any other sentence examined in this study for eliminating and [delaying] recidivism. On the other hand, sentences involving detention should be carefully considered in relating the types of delinquents they may be effective on. (Wooldredge, 1988, pp. 281, 293)

Juvenile Intensive Probation Supervision

The concept of intensive probation supervision (IPS) was one of a new generation of strategies to emerge from the intermediate sanctions movement. First developed for adult offenders, IPS programs were intended to both provide an alternative to incarceration for appropriate offenders as well as to enhance the impact of supervision on high-risk probationers.

The concept spread to the juvenile domain quickly and spawned similar experimentation, though not nearly on the same scale as the adult programs. The program models emphasized reduced caseloads and, in contrast to similar efforts in the 1960s, put a premium on closer surveillance and monitoring, with reduced attention to treatment (Armstrong, 1991).

As with so much else in the juvenile correctional field, little reliable scientific evidence is available on program impact. The National Council on Crime and Delinquency (NCCD) undertook a review of some 41 programs in the late 1980s and found that evaluative data of program sites was 'generally nonexistent' (Krisberg *et al.*, 1989, p. 40). A similar conclusion was reached by Armstrong (1991), who found only five scientifically acceptable program evaluations and further criticized the absence of any apparent theoretical basis for the programs.

Though useful research on juvenile IPS programs is scarce, two studies produced at least minimally reliable results. In the New Pride Replication Project, conducted between 1980 and 1984, ten newly established juvenile IPS programs were located in both medium and large cities. The program was comprised of two 6-month phases, the first involving near-daily contact which gradually decreased during the second phase. The programs supplemented this intensive supervision with heavy doses of alternative schooling, vocational training, and job placement. After gathering outcome data over three years, findings revealed no significant differences between the experiment and control groups (Palmer, 1992). Another study on three juvenile IPS programs using random assignment found comparable results, though it was asserted that the IPS cost less than one-third of the expense of incarceration.

More recently, an experiment was undertaken by the Toledo Juvenile Court in using IPS as a diversion from commitment to the state youth authority. Employing a mix of surveillance and treatment techniques, the program extended over 6 months, and the research employed an 18-month follow-up period. Results found that there was no difference in subsequent recidivism between the IPS youth and a matched group committed to the Ohio Department of Youth Services. Researchers concluded that the IPS program posed no greater threat to public safety, at approximately 20 per cent of the cost of incarcerating the same youth (Wiebush, 1993).

Violent Offenders

In light of the prospect of a growing number of violent juveniles, information specific to intervening with violent offenders is especially critical. Recent research includes one major evaluation of intensive supervision for violent juveniles, in which supervision focused on job placement, education and, to a lesser extent, family counseling and peer support. In a two-year follow-up measuring subsequent felony or violent arrests, no significant differences were found between program youth and a control group who were institutionalized for 8 months and then placed on standard juvenile parole. Some evidence was found that sites which had stronger and/or consistently implemented treatment components produced better results (Palmer, 1992). However, it must be stressed that participation in this program *followed* commitment to a small, secure juvenile facility for subsequent stays in community programs for several months. Consequently, it would be problematic to compare the study group's experience to that of most juvenile probationers.

Juvenile Boot Camp

Boot camps have become a popular option on the continuum of sanctions for adult offenders. Therefore, as with IPS programs, it is not surprising that juvenile agencies have implemented their own versions of boot camps. Such programs emphasize strong discipline, modeled on military programs and a strict physical conditioning regimen. The typical program is aimed at non-violent offenders, and involves a three-month commitment followed by after-care (Peterson, 1996).

In 1992, the US Justice Department's Office of Juvenile Justice and Delinquency Prevention (OJJDP) funded three new juvenile boot camps and undertook impact evaluations. The subsequent reports found that most participants completed the program and that academic skills were significantly improved. Furthermore, a significant number of participants found jobs during aftercare. However, no reduction in recidivism was found compared to a control group of juveniles who were institutionalized or placed on probation (Peterson, 1996).

Juvenile Transfer to Adult Court

One clear result of the growing violence committed by youth is an increased reliance on the 'transfer' option – that is, the power of the system to move jurisdiction over juvenile offenders into adult court, to take advantage of the greater penalties available at the adult level. The popularity of the transfer option is reflected in both an increased number of cases where jurisdiction is waived (a 41 per cent increase from 1989–93) as well as legislative reforms aimed at making waivers more automated than discretionary.

Studies conducted on the comparative effectiveness of handling similar offenders in adult versus juvenile court give the advantage to juvenile court where recidivism is the measure. Most studies indicate that juveniles imprisoned in adult facilities were more likely to be arrested following release.

In the making of criminal or juvenile justice policy, frequently political and ideological considerations will override (if not totally ignore) the available empirical data. The move to transfer a greater number of juvenile offenders to adult court is not likely to abate; it is a specific reform that has become captive of the 'get tough' philosophy that unquestionably holds sway in the current climate.

Rethinking the Standard for Success

All of the programs reviewed above represent the characteristic efforts at recent reform in juvenile corrections, and are alike in their emphasis on increased supervision of offenders, coupled in some instances (the more effective experiments) with increased rehabilitative services. They are also alike in having largely failed by the most important measure – recidivism.

Why has there been so little success? Ted Palmer, arguably the dean of research in juvenile corrections, argues that 'intensive' programs have not been intensive enough, in light of the multiple needs presented by high risk offenders: '[G]iven the interrelatedness of most serious, multiple offenders' difficulties and deficits, it is perhaps overly optimistic to expect fairly short-term programs to help most such individuals sort out and settle these matters once and for all, even if the programs are intensive' (Palmer, 1992, p. 112).

It may be that the system has been attempting to generate success on the cheap. Meeting expectations of turning very

troubled youth from confirmed pathways of negative and predatory behavior – patterns developed over perhaps a decade of poor,
if not harmful, rearing – through the application of concentrated
service for 6 to 12 months may be entirely unrealistic. To do the
impossible, we have generally spent less than one-third the cost
of institutionalizing these same youths.

Rather than congratulate ourselves for the short-term cost savings represented by diversion from incarceration to an intermediate sanction, we should think of making a substantial investment
in the near term – something, let us say, more equivalent to the
cost of a year's incarceration – in order to increase the chances of
long-term, significant savings being made on future imprison-
ments avoided. Americans, it has often been observed, are con-
genitally drawn to short-term strategies and quick returns on their
investment. What has been found not to work in other domains,
such as business or personal investment, may similarly prove
self-defeating in juvenile justice.

FIVE STEPS TOWARD REFORMED JUVENILE PROBATION

Let Research Drive Policy

Despite an ever-growing body of research relevant to the formation of criminal justice policy, it remains remarkable how little
empirical findings inform the design of programs in juvenile justice. As a result of this rather wilful ignorance, the juvenile probation field can be found to embrace existing models for
intervention (such as juvenile IPS) with scant evidence, if any,
that such models work. The field too often becomes enthralled
by the latest fad and rushes to adopt it, irrespective of the evidence that it has or can work. Finckenauer (1982) has referred to
this as the 'panacea phenomenon', and it seems no less common
17 years after he first identified this tendency.

This myopia on the part of correctional administrators has
multiple explanations. First, practitioners typically value the wis-
dom imparted by experience more than that contained in criminological journals. They prefer to consult their own intuition and

gut instincts rather than any hard data. Second, the pertinent research is not as accessible as it might be. This is a product of the conventions of the academy, which rewards publication in criminological journals more so than the publications practitioners commonly read or consult. Finally, administrators and policy-makers live and work in a politically charged atmosphere where 'what works' is only one of the relevant considerations in developing policy. In the administrator's world, that which is congruent with the current political climate may indeed depart from what makes sense empirically.

Even allowing for the burden to survive the ideological wars, juvenile probation administrators could do a much better job of incorporating a research perspective into their decision-making. This research-sensitive approach would take two forms. First, managers must realize that policy rarely needs to be created in a vacuum; that is, in setting policy in any particular direction there will usually be some data bearing on the decision to be made. Becoming familiar with the techniques for adequately researching the literature and accessing the federal information services is crucial, and requires the staffing of at least a modest research division.

Second, all new initiatives should include a strong evaluation component. We have missed opportunities to learn from much previous experimentation because data was not kept in a way that facilitated any useful analysis (Palmer, 1992). All new programs should be seen as experiments, with clearly demonstrated time-lines and methodologies for assessing impact. Juvenile probation agencies must become 'learning organizations' in which no course of action becomes institutionalized until its value is proven, and feedback loops should become a regular feature of the informational architecture of an agency (Senge, 1990).

Instead of viewing decisions about future programs as choices between 'tough' versus 'lenient', probation administrators should train themselves to think more in terms of 'smart' versus 'dumb'. Smart programs are those built on existing research with strong evaluation components. While not all programs sponsored by juvenile probation must meet this test absolutely (restitution programs are vital, irrespective of their impact on recidivism), juvenile probation will gain credibility and demonstrate greater impact as it gets smarter.

Emphasize Early Intervention

If juvenile probation were analogized to an investment strategy, the enterprise would be facing bankruptcy. In many respects, resources are allocated to that area (older, chronic offenders) where they are least likely to gain an impressive return. First offenders, by contrast, are all but ignored. Demonstrated incapacity for reform – not amenability to change – is what earns attention from the system. That must change.

Much has been learned in the past 20 years about the early precursors of chronic delinquency (Greenwood *et al.*, 1996). We have learned, for example, that children whose parents are cold, cruel and inconsistent in their parenting skills are at greatly increased risk for becoming enmeshed in the juvenile justice system.

So what? Is there anything that can be done about it? Yes: models have been developed that work dramatically in training parents to supervise more effectively their own children, reducing significantly later delinquencies. In a report released in 1996, Rand Corporation researchers identified forms of parent training that are among the two or three most cost-effective strategies in terms of reducing crime and delinquency (Greenwood *et al.*, 1996). An elaborate and highly tested model of this type of training, developed by the Oregon Social Learning Center, has been positively supported by repeated evaluations (Wilson, 1995b).

One collateral finding from this research – in fact, from nearly all research on prevention – is that intervening earlier (in or before the primary grades) yields stronger results. Most delinquents enter the juvenile court in their early teens. Can they be reached earlier?

Quite apart from what schools and other communities can do with younger children, juvenile courts have access to young children encountered either as the subject of abuse and neglect petitions or as younger siblings of older delinquents. By reconceptualizing their mandate as intervening with families instead of solely with the convicted juvenile, courts can truly enter the prevention business in a viable way. The Rand report strongly suggests that a small amount spent earlier on young children and their families can save much more substantial costs later. For example, in Los Angeles the Juvenile Court has undertaken a special project with first offenders who have the hallmarks of chronic delinquents. Instead of waiting for several arrests before intensive services are provided, the current guiding principle is that a greater investment earlier on makes more sense (Humes, 1996). This preventive approach promises to work better and cost less.

Intervening aggressively with abusive families would also very likely repay itself many times over. Juveniles found guilty of the more serious crimes typically have long histories of abuse. A National Institute of Justice study found that an abused or neglected child has a 40 per cent greater chance of becoming delinquent than other children (DiIulio, 1996). Assessment instruments are now available to determine the ongoing risk for abuse within families as well as to predict the likelihood that patterns of abuse will change once an intervention has commenced (Gelles, 1996). Focusing attention on abusive families will pay off both in terms of child protection and delinquency prevention.

Emphasize the Paying of Just Debts

The public image of the juvenile court has been marred for decades by the impression that it coddles vicious children and 'treats' kids who are more deserving of punishment. Probation administrators ignore this perception at their peril, as it undermines their credibility and diminishes public support. Both as a matter of justice and good correctional practice, juveniles should get their 'just deserts' for harm done. Restitution and community service programs repay and restore victims and harmed communities, in addition to countering the prevalent notion that juvenile offenders are immune from any real penalties, an impression certainly reinforced by Humes' (1996) recent study of the Los Angeles Juvenile Court. In his otherwise bleak and discouraging account, Humes relates the story of a program that places juvenile probationers in a school for disabled children where

the probationer must discharge his community service responsibilities by caring for and feeding young children with major
disabilities. A juvenile prosecutor described the impact of the
program as follows:

> These are street thugs, serious offenders, some of the worst
> kids who come through here. Most of them have served time in
> camp or at the Youth Authority, and they're harder than ever.
> Then they end up feeding and bathing autistic and wheelchair-
> bound kids, working with them intensively, having these hand-
> icapped folks depending on them utterly. It works a kind of
> magic. It softens them. For the first time in their lives, some-
> one is dependent on them. And it changes them. It's been going
> for four years, there's never been a problem, never anyone
> neglected or hurt. Rival gang members go there and work
> together side by side. Sometimes it seems like a miracle. (p. 173)

One of the most promising new paradigms in juvenile justice is
the 'Balanced and Restorative Justice Model' developed by
Gordon Bazemore of Florida Atlantic University and his colleagues. In a compelling design that attempts simultaneously to
serve the just expectations of victim, community and offender
alike, the following principle is enunciated: 'When an offense
occurs by the offender, an obligation incurs by the offender to
the victim that must be fulfilled' (Maloney and Umbreit, 1995,
p. 43). All juvenile probationers – in the interests of justice, for
the sake of any injured victims or communities, and, not insignif-
icantly, for their own moral education – must be compelled to
pay their just debts. In doing so, wounds heal, losses are restored,
and the moral sentiments of the community are assuaged.

Make Probation Character-Building

In the parlance of traditional clinical assessments, most delinquents
have been labeled as 'character-disordered'. To many observers,
this was a kind of 'default' diagnosis that filled in the blank when
no other form of mental illness seemed present. Indeed, delinquents do seem lacking in what we refer to commonly as character, by which we generally mean habits of thought and action that

reveal a fidelity to principles of integrity, good comportment, concern for others and self-control (Wilson, 1995b).

Neo-conservative perspectives on crime have brought the issue of character defects among delinquents and criminals to the foreground, in contrast to the medical model which attributed various 'problems' and 'illnesses' to offenders, deficiencies presumably beyond their control and therefore beyond their responsibility (Wilson, 1995a). Imparting bad character to delinquents would seem to imply greater responsibility for wrongdoing while also pointing to a different type of remediation.

Can a term of juvenile probation build character? As Wilson (1995b) suggests, we know little about how to inculcate character. Yet we have some clues. According to Aristotle, character is reflected not in some inner quality or virtue, but in a pattern of commendable actions which, in the doing, both build and reveal character. In the Aristotelian sense, then, juvenile courts can attempt to build character by compelling probationers to complete actions that youth of high character would undertake. Compensating for harm done, discussed above, is surely part of this. Regular attendance and good behavior at school would also reflect character in action. Obeying the reasonable requests of parents, and respectable conduct at home and in the neighborhood, would further exemplify character. If Aristotle was right that we become good by doing good, requiring juvenile probationers to do good even though they may not seem or yet be good could, over time, build what we call character.

As Andrews *et al.* (1986) found, effective probation officers model pro-social behavior. Juvenile probation officers must then see themselves as moral educators, who must constantly look for opportunities to exemplify good character to those they supervise. Every occasion where self-restraint is exercised in the face of a probationer's provocation, where kindness and courtesy is extended to a probationer's family in defiance of the juvenile's expectation, and every effort by the officer to insure fair treatment in dispositional and revocational proceedings is an opportunity for character building and moral education.

If character is revealed in making moral decisions, then juvenile probation agencies could undertake more explicit strategies for moral development. Though more employed in educational than correctional settings, techniques for instilling a heightened moral sense have been used successfully in advancing the moral reasoning powers of young children (Lickona, 1991). Based on Lawrence Kohlberg's highly regarded theory of moral development, participants in the program are led through discussions of moral dilemmas where they must reconcile competing interests and reach just solutions. Research has shown that subjects can elevate their moral reasoning away from more selfish egocentric perspectives to broader, more altruistic and empathetic thinking.

This psycho-educational strategy would lend itself readily to the probation environment. In lieu of what is too often a rather mechanical and vacuous exchange with a probation officer once or twice each month, young offenders could participate in discussion groups led by trained probation officers with both offenders and staff probably feeling that they are engaged in a more productive experience.

Prioritize Violence Prevention

In light of the growing rates of serious juvenile violence, and with this trend expected to continue into the next decade (Fox, 1996), juvenile probation must focus on suppressing violent behavior. As mentioned earlier, there is scant evidence that the more punitive strategies will have long-term impact (it must be said that there are independent 'just deserts' rationales for punishing seriously violent offenders, but this does not account for first offenders showing aggressive tendencies). Again drawing from efforts more commonly found in schools, some juvenile probation departments, such as that of Massachusetts, have undertaken violence-prevention programs with juvenile probationers. These programs employ curricula designed to improve the social, problem-solving and anger management skills of young offenders. While curricula vary, most employ an interactive, exercise-based, skill-building model that extends over an average of 10 to 15 sessions of an hour or so's duration.

Evaluations conducted on such programs indicate that they are generally effective in improving social skills (Brewer and

Gardner, 1996). An evaluation of a program undertaken with juvenile probationers in Massachusetts demonstrated significant reductions in subsequent juvenile violence (Romano, 1996). More importantly, this program, sponsored by the Boston Juvenile Court for several years now, attests to the viability of such programming within the juvenile probation context.

Given the aforementioned growth in juvenile violence attributed to firearms, prevention programs targeted on this area warrant consideration. Unfortunately, very little has been done: 'Programs that intervene with young people who use guns or have been caught with guns unfortunately are rare and in dire need of further development' (OJJDP, 1996, p. 16). None the less, initiating more efforts in this area makes sense. Studies of handgun possession by youth indicate that handguns are more likely to be owned by individuals with a prior record of violent behavior, particularly where the gun is illegal (OJJDP, 1996). This suggests a real potential pay-off in targeting juvenile probationers.

Firearm-prevention programs have been undertaken in several juvenile jurisdictions, although little evaluative information is available. Arizona's Pima County Juvenile Court, for example, operates a course for youth who, though not chronic offenders, are before the court for offenses involving the carrying or firing of a gun, or have been identified as being at risk for firearm use. Parents are required to attend these educational sessions, where the law governing gun use and the dangers implicit in unauthorized use are explained (OJJDP, 1996).

Given the extent of the violence problem, further experimentation and evolution seems highly warranted. Moreover, a greater reliance on substantive group-work modalities offers a sensible alternative to the traditional and exhausted model of one-on-one contact, cynically derided within the profession as 'fifteen minutes of avoiding eye contact once a month'.

THE PROSPECTS AHEAD

The five reforms recommended above constitute a modest and therefore achievable agenda. They would probably not entail additional large expenditures, but would rely on reallocating existing resources and redeploying current staff. Implementing them would not deliver utopian, crime-free communities in the next millennium, but we have reason to believe they would be worth the effort.

Progressive administrators will no doubt consider such initiatives, in addition to others not mentioned here. As to the rest, a changing climate in governmental circles may compel the reluctant and unimaginative to undertake steps toward building a system both more effective and more congruent with public attitudes and expectations (Corbett, 1996). In the face of disturbing projections in future rates of youthful violence, immediate action does not seem premature.

REFERENCES

Andrews, D. A. and Gendreau, P. (1990) Tertiary prevention: What the meta-analyses of the offender treatment literature tells us about 'what works'. *Canadian Journal of Criminology* 32, 173–84.

Andrews, D., Kiessling, J., Robinson, D. and Mickus, S. (1986) The risk principle of case classification: An outcome evaluation with young adult probationers. *Canadian Journal of Criminology* 28, 377–84.

Armstrong, T. L. (ed.) (1991) Introduction. *Intensive Interventions with High Risk Youths* (pp. 1–26). Monsey, New York: Criminal Justice Press.

Blumstein, A. (1996) *Youth Violence, Guns, and Illicit Drug Markets*. Washington, DC: National Institute of Justice.

Brewer, M. B. and Gardner, W. (1996) Who is this 'we'? Levels of collective identity and self representations. *Journal of Personality and Social Psychology* 71, 83–93.

Butterfield, F. (1996) After 10 years, juvenile crime begins to drop. *The New York Times* (9 August).

Corbett, R. P., Jr. (1996) When community corrections means business: Introducing 'reinventing' themes to probation and parole. *Federal Probation* 60, 36–42.

Council on Crime in America (1996) *The State of Violent Crime in America*. Washington, DC: Council on Crime in America.

DiIulio, J. J., Jr. (1996) Stop crime where it starts. *The New York Times* (31 July), A15.

Finckenauer, J. (1982) *Scared straight! and the panacea phenomenon.* Englewood Cliffs, New Jersey: Prentice Hall.

Fox, J. A. (1996) *Trends In Juvenile Violence – A Report to the United States Attorney General on Current and Future Rates of Juvenile Offending.* Washington, DC: Bureau of Justice Statistics, United States Department of Justice.

Gelles, R. J. (1996) *The Book of David.* New York: Basic Books.

Gendreau, P. (1996) The principles of effective intervention with offenders. In A. T. Harland (ed.), *Choosing Correctional Options That Work* (pp. 117–30). Thousand Oaks, California: Sage Publications.

Greenwood, P. W., Model, K., Rydell, C. P. and Chiesa, J. (1996) *Diverting Children From A Life of Crime.* Santa Monica, California: RAND.

Humes, E. (1996) *No Matter How Loud I Shout.* New York: Simon & Schuster.

Jacobs, M. D. (1990) *Screwing the System and Making It Work.* Chicago: University of Chicago Press.

Lickona, T. (1991) *Educating For Character.* New York: Bantam Books.

Lipsey, M. W. (1995) What do we learn from 400 research studies on the effectiveness of treatment with juvenile delinquents? In J. McGuire (ed.), *What Works. Reducing Reoffending: Guidelines from Research Practices* (pp. 63–78). Chichester, England: John Wiley & Sons.

Krisberg, B., Rodriguez, O., Baake, A., Nuenfeldt, D. and Steele, P. (1989) *Demonstration of Post-adjudication, Non-residential Intensive Supervision Programs: Assessment Report.* San Francisco: National Council on Crime and Delinquency.

Maloney, D. M. and Umbreit, M. S. (1995) Managing change: Toward a balanced and restorative justice model. *Perspectives* (Spring), 43–6.

National Center for Juvenile Justice (1991) *Desktop Guide to Good Juvenile Probation Practice.* Pittsburgh: National Juvenile Court Services Association.

OJJDP (Office of Juvenile Justice and Delinquency) (1996) *Reducing Youth Gun Violence: An Overview of Programs and Initiatives.* Washington, DC: Office of Justice Programs.

Palmer, T. (1992) *The Re-Emergence of Correctional Intervention.* Thousand Oaks, California: Sage Publications.

Petersilia, J. (1991) Policy relevance and the future of criminology. *Criminology* 29, 1–15.

Peterson, E. (1996) *Juvenile Boot Camps: Lessons Learned.* Washington, DC: Office of Juvenile Justice and Delinquency Prevention.

Romano, L. (1996) *Preliminary Evaluation Report: Violence Prevention Groups.* Newton, Massachusetts: Romano & Associates.

Senge, P. M. (1990) *The Fifth Discipline.* New York: DoubleDay Currency.

Sheindlin, J. (1996) *Don't Pee On My Leg and Tell Me It's Raining.* New York: Harper Collins Publishers, Inc.

Snyder, H. N., Sickmund, M. and Poe-Yamagata, E. (1996) *Juvenile Offenders and Victims: 1996 Update on Violence.* Washington, DC: Office of Juvenile Justice and Delinquency Prevention.

Torbet, P. M. (1996) *Juvenile Probation: The Workhorse of the Juvenile Justice System.* Washington, DC: Office of Juvenile Justice and Delinquency Prevention.

Wiebush, R. G. (1993) Juvenile intensive supervision: The impact on felony offenders diverted from institutional placement. *Crime & Delinquency* 39, 68–89.

Wilson, J. Q. (1995a) Crime and public policy. In J. Q. Wilson and J. Petersilia (eds.), *Crime*. San Francisco: CS Press.

——. (1995b) *On Character*. Washington, DC: AEI Press.

Wooldredge, J. (1988) Differentiating the effects of juvenile court sentences on eliminating recidivism. *Journal of Research in Crime and Delinquency* 25, 264–300.

8 The Center of Concern: Crime and the Family

Patricia Morgan

Haven't we been here before? I get that sense of *déjà vu* each time I read another evaluation of some 'innovative' rehabilitative program for juvenile delinquents. One just reviewed was designed to determine whether delinquents, newly released from residential placements and assigned to an intensive aftercare experiment, had lower recidivism rates and a better readjustment to their communities than youth given regular post-release supervision by social workers and probation officers (Greenwood, Deschenes and Adams, 1993). The 12-month follow-up showed a decline in coping skills and no significant impact on arrests, self-reported delinquency, or alcohol or drug use in the treatment group. Another program involved a comprehensive and structured array of services and activities, to determine if youths convicted of serious offenses behave better after release than when assigned to traditional training schools. At one-year follow-up there were no significant differences between the experimental and control groups (Greenwood and Turner, 1993). The third program, run by Michigan social services, combined three months' residence in the wilderness with nine months of intensive community-based aftercare. Early analyses suggest that between 40 and 50 per cent of youth are failing in the community phase, with about 25 per cent being placed in training schools and another 20 per cent having gone missing (Deschenes, Greenwood and Adams, 1994).

There seems no limit to the triumph of hope over experience. Two decades ago, Robert Martinson summarized the results of well over 200 separate attempts to rehabilitate offenders, from a massive tome commissioned by the New York State Governor's Committee on Criminal Offenders. The finding was that 'with few and isolated exceptions, the rehabilitative efforts that have been reported so far have had no appreciable effect on recidivism'

(Martinson, 1974; Lipton, Martinson and Wilks, 1975). Others had already come to similar conclusions, undermining all the mythology about the effectiveness of any treatment for offenders (Bailey, 1971; Wilkins, 1969; Greenberg, 1977). Some attempts, involving the intensive therapeutic and permissive regimes encouraged by the 1969 Children and Young Persons Act in the United Kingdom, seemed to make offenders worse. Certainly, Kingswood therapeutic community failed dismally compared to other environments, with its reconviction rate of 70 per cent even after having been allowed to hand-pick the less aggressive, more intelligent and emotionally stable boys for its program (Cornish and Clarke, 1975; Brody, 1976).

The rash of expensive experiments in the 1960s and 1970s promised to reverse the depressing trend to higher and higher rates of reconviction. Since the 1950s there had been a sharp decline in the 'success' rates of institutions and programs dealing with delinquents. The 60 per cent of the mid-1950s had collapsed to 34 per cent by the late 1960s, and was down to around 30 per cent by the mid-1970s. At the same time the big upsurge in delinquency and crime was also under way, and the rehabilitationists failed to see how this boded ill for claims about reversing the trend to higher and higher recidivism rates. It is not surprising that 'nothing works':

> It requires not merely optimistic but heroic assumptions about the nature of man to lead one to suppose that a person, finally sentenced after (in most cases) many brushes with the law ... should, by either the solemnity of prison or the skillfulness of a counselor, come to see the error of his ways and to experience a transformation of his character. Today we smile in amusement at the naïveté of those early prison reformers who imagined that religious instruction while in solitary confinement would lead to moral regeneration. How they would smile at us at our presumption that conversations with a psychiatrist or a return to the community could achieve the same end. (Wilson, 1983, p. 165)

'People-changing' cannot succeed: the assumptions behind rehabilitation are all wrong. We are not just products of our environment, but are sustained by it. We adjust to the present as much as we are shaped by the past (Morgan, 1978). The researchers who carried out the Kingswood study got to the heart of the matter by observing that

> the persistence in criminal behavior of certain individuals, despite the treatment they are given and the measures taken against them, may largely be accounted for by the fact that there is little change in the environments which they normally inhabit. (Cornish, 1975)

If changes in behavior or attitudes are not supported in everyday life, the likelihood is that these will not last. No intervention, no regime, no treatment will do much to change the rates of recidivism if the outside society does not bring pressures to bear upon individuals to behave constructively in normal life. They make the situation worse, when the law abandons what it *can* do. This is to deter, as well as to mark the distinction between right and wrong by a just proportion between deed and disposal, and to educate by reinforcing the norms which people must themselves uphold. Otherwise, what grows is the fear, confusion, and demoralization which occurs in society when offenses go unpunished or are punished disproportionately.

The tremendous rise in recidivism rates for all institutions and regimes has the same cause as the general rise in lawbreaking among young people and children, and the corresponding rise in adult crime since the 1950s – that society has become generally more conducive to lawbreaking compared to the previous half-century or more. Or rather, it is to be concluded that the social pressures which kept a child and young person from lawbreaking in the first place, which prevented adults committing crimes, and which worked for the 'spontaneous remission' of the delinquent behavior of actual lawbreakers as they got older, have generally diminished over recent decades.

It almost goes without saying that much that comes under the rubric of criminality is ubiquitous in human society and part of the mundane repertoire of normality. As observed by Travis Hirschi, we do not inherit crime (although some may inherit more than the average share of propensities conducive to such behavior). Nor need we learn crime – although some may, because crime usually presupposes little or no knowledge, skill, or effort that is not routinely available to all. Delinquency is especially consistent with youth recreational patterns, in providing immediate gratification, excitement, risks, and thrills (Hirschi, 1995). The perennial problems of control necessitate the continuous exposition and maintenance of norms. Without restraints, individuals will tend to follow their own, often short-term interests, to the detriment of others and eventually themselves. Social order is a fragile contrivance, not a spontaneous creation.

However, many modern rehabilitative endeavors have often been attempts to undo or make good whatever might be blamed for thwarting or warping the individual's otherwise natural and wholesome growth to maturity. This is all tied to assumptions that, given the right background conditions, nobody goes wrong and that this somehow allows us to dispense with ties, rules, and corrections, since individuals thrive best when least incumbered by external constraints. As Hirschi (1983, p. 54) asserts, in terms of 'modern' theories of crime, which 'assume that the individual would be noncriminal were it not for the operation of unjust and misguided institutions', explanations that focus on the family are particularly 'contrary to the metaphysic of our age'. This offers the possibility of a society which spontaneously orders itself when all 'need' is met or, in T. S. Eliot's words, a system 'so perfect that no-one will need to be good'. Indeed, institutions such as the family are arbitrary arrangements that limit the potential and freedom of individuals and, as such, may be the source of the problem. Certainly, strong families are persistently saddled 'with the sins of weak families' (for example, child abuse), and workers in the system also promote 'child-rearing practices at best orthogonal (that is, unconnected) to the practices suggested by research on delinquency' (Hirschi, 1995, p. 139).

The progressive mindset finds it particularly offensive that the connection between the family and crime is implicitly dependent on a connection between morality and crime. As Hirschi explains, the family as such is not associated directly with crime, but is associated with moral issues, or with divorce, desertion, illegitimacy, adultery, or promiscuity (Hirschi, 1995). These are threatening to the family, and their acceptance will reflect its declining strength, with theft, violence, and vandalism thriving on its weaknesses. If people are free to behave in ways inconsistent with or potentially damaging to the family, this deprives the community of the interlocking alliances and intergenerational bonds produced by marriage and parenthood.

For long now, much of the criminological industry has been in the business of producing explanations, often highly esoteric and convoluted, in terms of environmental constraints, deficiencies, or exposure to stressful influences, including race and class discrimination. Where they are recognized, differences in criminality between families may be seen in terms of inadvertent differences in exposure to criminal influences outside of the family. Similarities in the criminal behavior of parents and children are put down to subculture or neighborhood. The structure or working of the family itself is irrelevant, and support for the family hardly a goal of policy. As there is nothing in the institution of the family that cannot be provided by other means, it is believed that whatever problems are thrown up by its weakness, contraction, and fragmentation can be dealt with by professional agencies and financial support. In so far as the moral issues represented by the family have little or nothing to do with the penal concerns of the state, the family and crime exist in different domains.

This has been despite the evidence that offenders from neglectful and broken families have always been heavily over-represented in the criminal justice and penal system – although this can be interpreted as bias in the system. However, while Hirschi sees academics as now more willing to accept that the major determinant of arrest, conviction, and imprisonment is the behavior of the offender, family disruption continues to be the 'black sheep' of criminological research. One result of this is that the criminological significance of the major indicators of family weakness, like divorce and illegitimacy, remain the focus of considerable skepticism, if not scorn. What Norman Dennis and George Erdos have recently done, to much consternation, in *Families without Fatherhood*, is to reunite crime with the traditional moral problems of the family (Dennis and Erdos, 1992).

A control theory of crime has to assume that decent behavior must be 'somehow built in through socialization and maintained by the threat of sanctions', which unavoidably puts the family at the heart of the matter, just as a family-based explanation of crime is bound to take a control position (Hirschi, 1983, p. 54). If what children must learn is self-control, the ability to resist temptations of the moment in favor of long-term projects or prospects, then this socialization primarily rests with the family, and research and policy must concentrate on child-rearing and family structure to understand crime and reduce its frequency. Such research does, after all, have a considerable pedigree, as well as consistent findings. We are reminded that, back in 1950, Sheldon and Eleanor Glueck reported that they were able to predict delinquency from an early age using five factors of family background: supervision of boys by mother or father, affection for boys by mother and father, and the cohesiveness of the family – not much different from those of Gerald Paterson and his colleagues at the Oregon Social Learning Center in the 1980s (Glueck and Glueck, 1950; Hirschi, 1995; see also Sampson and Laub, 1993, for a recent re-analysis of the Glueck data in support of their theory of informal social control).

However, in the intervening years control theory has tended to be dismissed as 'outdated' and the exponents marginalized as vulgar, repressive bumpkins who pander to populism. But has not the public been right? Do not delinquency and crime largely reflect lowered levels of self-control? Is not right conduct a matter of attitudes, rules, and constraints (Gottfredson and Hirschi, 1990)? These are shaped and maintained in youth ties to family, friends, neighborhood, school, and workplace; and it is here that the rules and values must be taught and, in turn, enforced, which run counter to violent, destructive, and dishonest behavior. Unavoidably, ineffective child-rearing is a prime cause of low levels of self-control. The extent of the child's relationships with adults, his involvement and the salience of his ties, are – as his stakes in society – the measure of his integration. And, of these relationships, the family is the foremost educative influence which fits its members for citizenship in the wider community.

Moreover, it is not just that the family happens to be strategically placed to mold and control the conduct of the growing individual, given that socialization is scarcely separable from procreation. And, following on from this, it is not simply that no values could be viable unless they were taken up and passed within families. There is also the consideration of moral origins. Family life implies a particular responsibility, involving the suspension of self-interest for the sake of others, reciprocity and binding obligations. While this 'compulsory altruism' is brought into play by the demands of family life, its generalization supports other institutions – providing the mutual trust, loyalty, and solidarity which underpins social control everywhere (Fortes, 1983). As the template of society, the family both teaches and embodies those values which, in the wider context, animate civilized communities (Sacks, 1995).

This is not to insist that there is any determinism involved in either process. The socialization enterprise may fail or break down at one or any number of points for a variety of reasons: the parents may not care for the child and, even if they do, they may not have the time or energy to monitor the child's behavior. They may not see anything wrong with the child's behavior, or they may not have the means or inclination to punish the child (Hirschi, 1995). In turn, the degree and nature of the application of 'family values' to other social relations varies enormously over time and place (and has been limited in some societies).

Michael Rutter and David J. Smith, in a lengthy analysis of the surge in psychosocial disorders among the young since the 1950s, now vindicate those who have been trying to point to changes in the nature of upbringing as causes of the upsurge in delinquency in these years (Rutter and Smith, 1995). The impetus behind the tenfold rise in crime in Britain, committed mostly by young people, and paralleled by other sudden and unprecedented upward trends in drug and alcohol abuse, suicidal behavior, depression, and eating disorders, is increased freedom and independence, as adults have permissively withdrawn from protective and educative roles. Beginning in the 'golden age' of low unemployment and rising living standards, it has been greatly intensified by the development of an isolated youth culture, which further serves to isolate adolescents.

The abandonment of confused young people to a moral vacuum in the postwar world has been very much at the instigation of influential 'expert' élites. Their child-rearing advice directly challenged the family's socialization role. In their child-centered ethos, the adult responds to the child's inherent needs. He is the enabler of a self-determined process of unfolding development, in which the child is the agent of his own upbringing, and in which moral principles and character formation give way to personality and personal expression (to which we must now add 'sexuality'). Where once the child 'was thought to be endowed by nature with dangerous impulses that must be curbed, now he was seen as equipped with harmless instincts that ought to be developed' (Wilson, 1983, p. 236). Strictures of right and wrong, good and bad, were not simply condemned as pre-scientific and outmoded, but productive of manifold pathologies.

What was being promulgated were the child-rearing practices of the classic slum. Had not an older generation of criminologists who studied what were then the remaining pockets of deviance in the 'criminal areas' of the big cities pointed to the low involvement of children with adults? And had they not drawn attention to adults who left the welfare of their large broods to the dubious influence of the peer group, with all its limitations as a humanizing and socializing agency?

Hard on the heels of the new child-rearing, the family itself came under assault as the 'traumatic collision finally occurred in the late 1960s between the new imperatives of expressiveness and the old culture of order and control' (Martin, 1981). The attack was precisely encapsulated at the moment it was launched in Britain by Dr Edmund Leach in his 1967 Reith Lectures for the BBC. The family was 'the source of all our discontents', and one of our fundamental troubles that 'we take it for granted that there is something intrinsically virtuous about law and order'.

The nuclear family was castigated as an institution guilty of the abuse of power and the suppression of liberty. The binding and imperative nature of family commitments appeared as intolerable impositions and impediments to personal choice, self-fulfilment, and autonomy. The foundation of love, dependence, and altruism in human life became the origin of oppression. The vehicle of cultural transmission became the perpetuator of a rotten social order. This onslaught on the family is indivisible from the assertion of the supremacy of individual self-expression, gratification, and unrestricted personal liberty as the pervading ethos – depriving society of patterns of sentiment, values, and action which are distinct to the family domain.

That infamous family is now subject to unprecedented disintegrative developments – not perhaps unconnected with the way in which its legal and economic foundations have been seriously eroded. Concomitant with this deinstitutionalization, the mother–child unit has increasingly become the focus of policy and support. What would have been received with alarm, even as a crisis, in the past, considering the impact on social cohesion, identity and continuity, has been accepted with equanimity, and even acclaimed as the rise of 'new family forms'. However, behind the semantic obfuscation is the contraction and fragmentation of the only family system we have known for centuries and are ever likely to know. While the majority of children are still with two natural and married parents, this norm is becoming less common; and the 'new families', which are being ushered in to replace the conjugal family, amount to informal unions or cohabitation, marriage breakdown, single motherhood, and childlessness. With half of men still unmarried at 30, the type of household which is growing most rapidly in the UK contains a single, childless man. By 2016, as one-person households grow from 27 per cent today to 37 per cent – having already climbed from 14 per cent in 1961 – 54 per cent of men aged 30 to 34 will be on their own. They are a reflection of the fact that there are now fewer first marriages than there were 100 years ago, despite the population having increased by three-quarters.

While the new, leaner generations are proportionately more the product of fatherlessness and broken relationships, it is also contrary to the 'metaphysic of our age' to interest oneself in the implications of this for children and society. Suggestions of differences in outcome for children from different home backgrounds are perceived as challenges to the validity of 'new family forms', or personal insults or affronts to those who have 'opted' for 'alternatives'. However, it should be clear that neither the demographic prevalence of the conjugal, nuclear family, nor the degree to which it is recognized or denied as a reality, or whether it is acclaimed or execrated as an ideal, alters the fact that conditions may differ in the consequences.

Raising a child is difficult enough under any circumstances, and it is not unreasonable to suppose that it might be more prone to problems when someone tries to do it alone. In terms of the simple arithmetic of relationships, parental attention is, on average, likely to be more attenuated. As such, the dilution of attention is also likely to be behind the finding that children in large families do not, on the whole, do so well at school or when it comes to staying out of trouble. As Sara McLanahan, authority on lone parenthood, emphasizes: 'whatever their capacities for managing their children, a couple can gang up on a teenager; a single parent cannot' (McLanahan, 1988, p. 20). Indeed, with fewer people socially obliged to lend support, the children of lone mothers are going to be progressively undercapitalized as this passes through more than one generation. In turn, the fission in the nucleus of the family comes on the heels of a decline or demise in other arrangements which once involved adults closely interacting with younger people. I am thinking particularly of the way that working-class boys often passed out of parental control only to come immediately under other forms of adult supervision and tutelage in the workplace, or in apprenticeships.

Especially at the poorest levels, a resident father is a significant barrier to a child being taken or received into institutional care (Marsh, 1987). Investigations suggest that three out of four children entering local authority care in Britain have lone parents (Bebbington and Miles, 1989). This is particularly significant when it is considered how those who have been in care are heavily represented among homeless and penal populations, where nearly 40 per cent of young people in custody in Britain have experience with the care system (Home Office, Research and Statistics Department, 1991). Performance deficiencies are caused as much by factors like parental inattention, conflict and stress, as by spending time in institutions or foster homes (Essen, Lambert and Head, 1976). This information is mirrored elsewhere. Seventy per cent of juveniles and young persons in US correctional institutions did not live with both parents while growing up (Bureau of Justice Statistics, 1988). Disrupted home backgrounds also contribute to as many as three in four teenage suicides and four in five psychiatric admissions (Council on Families in America, 1995).

Anyone reading the recent British study of persistent young offenders would be hard put to ignore that 15 per cent of these were living with neither parent, 5 per cent with their fathers only, 32 per cent with their mothers only and only 22 per cent living with what is described as two parents, but including step-parents, mother's boyfriends and grandparents (Hagell and Newburn, 1994). Furthermore, the degree of family disruption in the lives of persistent young offenders is said to be under-represented, since those with the most chaotic lives are so difficult for interviewers to find (156 out of an original sample of 251 were uncontactable or untraced).

It is possible to object to the connections suggested here, since we are reading backwards and so do not know about all the people that came from equally disturbed backgrounds, but did not become delinquent. However, the main British study to date of delinquent development, or the Cambridge Study, found future delinquents to be more likely to have been born illegitimate, and to have experienced broken homes or separations from parents other than those due to death or hospitalization (West, 1982). There was a doubling of the risk of delinquency where homes were broken by divorce. Data from the National Child Development Study, the main longitudinal study of child development in Britain, is frequently referred to in reviews of the outcomes for children of different backgrounds. What is likely to be missing is the finding from the 16-year-old follow-up that, while 8 per cent of boys with both natural parents had been to court at some time, the figure was 16 per cent for those with lone mothers and 19 per cent for boys with stepfathers. The figures for those who had dealings with police or probation officers were, respectively, 9 per cent, 17 per cent and 20 per cent (Ferri, 1984). Such findings have remained remarkably constant over time. Work on the criminal records of the earlier 1946 birth cohort of the National Survey of Health and Development showed how boys who had been through marital breakdown were more likely to be in custody, and those who had been young at the time of the break were twice as likely to be delinquent by the age of 21 and to have been convicted of serious offenses (Wadsworth, 1979, p. 115). The connections are reinforced by observations from intact families, like those of John and Elizabeth Newson (1982), on children growing up in Nottingham. Father involvement in middle and late childhood encouraged educational achievement and career plans, as well as preventing later lawlessness – surpassing any relationship with disciplinary styles or temperament.

Given the research now available, it is simply not good enough for those in a position to shape opinion and influence policy to keep insisting that family background is not associated with differences in behavior or achievement, or that the 'weight of evidence suggests that [the recorded] differences are due to the material circumstances of the families in question' (Coote, Harman and Hewitt, 1990, p. 29).

Nor is it good enough to exploit ignorance about the status of findings in social science to suggest that recorded differences between groups are sentences on all children in a category to do badly and, at the same time, that they have got to be wrong – because the adverse effect is not present in 100 per cent of the children exposed to particular conditions. In social science we are not in the business of looking for strict, exceptionless laws, as in physics, but probabilities, or that something will occur at a significantly higher rate in one group compared to another, and not because of accident or chance. To dismiss findings because there are exceptions is to demand impossible standards that would abolish social and medical investigation altogether.

There is usually no problem finding some ambiguous study or one that is contrary to the rest. Science is full of one-off experiments. In social science, the significant unit of research is the progressive series of studies and the convergence of results. In Britain the study which is now so often used to clinch the matter and rout the rest, or which is given disproportionate weight, is one done for the Home Office in 1985 on parental supervision and delinquency. This study found no difference in self-reported delinquency in the previous 12 months on the part of teenagers from one- and two-parent families (Riley and Shaw, 1985). But then it also failed to find any relationship between delinquency and any other measure of the family's economic or social difficulty or stress – whether low social class, unemployment, large family, or rough neighborhood – all of which have often been correlated with lawbreaking in other studies. Regrettably, it did not distinguish either between widowhood and lone parenthood as a result of other causes, or between two original parents and step-parents, when we know from elsewhere how important these variations are for outcomes. What it did find, however, was that delinquency was strongly associated with a lack of involvement or positive feelings between fathers and teenage children.

However, the following Home Office study, undertaken to provide an estimate of the extent, frequency, and nature of self-reported offending among 14- to 25-year-olds in England and Wales and to establish why some young people start to offend, confirmed that the proportion of offenders among those who did not get on well with their father was double that of those who had a good relationship with fathers. It also repeated the fact that, for both sexes, those who lived with both natural parents were less likely to offend than those with one parent, while those with step-parents were the most likely to offend (Graham and Bowling, 1995).

As the outcomes for different groups do overlap, and as the variables involved in child-rearing, like supervision, affection, parental aspirations and so forth, cross all family backgrounds, it is tempting to think that we have found some formula or device which renders questions of family structure irrelevant. We can disaggregate this into 'parenting processes' (Utting, Bright and Henricson, 1993). This seems to hold out the tempting prospect that families can become as fluid as the adults desire without adverse consequences. It does not matter how much relationships are dissolved and reconstituted, or how many men pass through the home, as long as the 'parenting' ingredients are supplied at the requisite level.

As pointed out elsewhere, family structure is a proxy for those factors that directly affect children's well-being. As well as family type, economic status or poverty is also structural, but its effects depend upon intervening variables – although those who condemn references to family structure are often the same people who resort to simplistic economic explanations. Decreased attention, affection, supervision, and communication are the characteristics of the relations that accompany marital dissolution or intermittent cohabitation, or reflect the task overload of single parents. A lone parent may be less capable of providing supervision, and *if* poor supervision is linked to delinquency then there is an unavoidable link between disrupted families and criminality.

The presence of other adults, like grandparents, brings household control levels closer to those of the two-parent family; so, by the same token, 'the raising of adolescents is not a task that can easily be borne by the mother alone' (Dornbusch *et al.*, 1985, p. 340). Moreover, variables like affection and even supervision – unless this refers simply to chaperonage – are affected by attachments. Those who speak of 'processes' almost suggest that it hardly matters who provides these, as long as they are supplied at the requisite level from one source or another, so that the making and breaking of significant relationships is irrelevant. But John Tripp and Monica Cockett from Exeter University in England (1994) have now found, as did Judith Wallerstein and Joan Kelly long before in California (1980; see also Wallerstein and Blakeslee, 1989), that it is family reorganization, particularly involving the father's departure, which is the leading adverse factor in the lives of children involved in marital breakup. The devastating psychological toll on children imposed by the absence or departure of a parent, rather than financial hardship or marital conflict, is what leads to poor health and adverse educational and social effects. The more transitions children experienced, the poorer the outcomes. Moreover, it is virtually axiomatic that attachment to parents is going to become attenuated and affectionate involvement reduced when non-resident fathers have little contact with their children, mothers are concentrating on their own interests and relationships, and stepfathers are not inclined to invest time and resources in other men's children.

One of the most sophisticated analyses dealing with delinquent outcomes, which helps us understand many other findings, is the work of Ross Matsueda and Karen Heimer (1987). Here, variables like parental supervision, attachment to peers, and attitudes to delinquency may be seen as aspects of social control and association, which depend upon family and social background just as broken homes, socio-economic status and neighborhood do. Living in a troubled neighborhood or a broken home is likely to weaken parental supervision, and low supervision increases delinquent peer relations, pro-delinquent attitudes and, ultimately, delinquent behavior. However, broken homes foster pro-delinquent attitudes in ways that cannot be explained simply in terms of supervision, because moral beliefs and attachments are also involved. As attachment facilitates supervision and discipline, so troubled neighborhoods and broken homes both dilute the ties to parents, reduce the strength of conventional beliefs, and increase the number of delinquent friends, compared to situations in which youth have warm relationships in intact families.

There may be much to be said for improving parenting skills. But it is not always possible to get some kinds of homes to function as well as others. To make the mother–child unit 'fully functional', or enable mothers to 'go it alone', we are now seeing lists for the most extensive and complex of remedial provisions, or compensatory measures, often as substitutes and supports for what the two-parent family is more likely to provide as a matter of course. As the state moves in to take upon itself the missing parents' functions, and to make good the loss of social capital for the children, it will have to assume these roles, when it is highly dubious how it could ever discharge such responsibilities adequately. Much may be beyond the reach of the most ambitious welfare services; moreover, these would have to be continually extended as a greater proportion of children enter groups associated with higher risk.

Adolescence is the time that juvenile activity becomes most difficult for adults to monitor and control. Here too it is often uncritically accepted that much of the role of families could be handed directly to professional agencies, to provide the teenage complements of the daycare for the under-fives and the children's centers, holiday activity schemes, and after-school containers for children. Together they all represent a major shift of personal services into the public domain so that, for family and kin, people have 'multi-agency outreach workers' and provide 'windows of opportunity' for counseling and intensive health-visiting programs.

Yet it is difficult to see how any number of statutory services could substitute for a general thinning of the number of responsible adults in the community. In disorganized communities, people's ties are few and disjointed. There is proximity, but little else. Society is a heap of building bricks, instead of a network of overlapping and supportive interdependencies (Suttles, 1968). Marital and family disruption reduce the linkages in the networks of social control as well as social support – dependent as this is on more than the individual child's family. It is easier for two parents to act when it comes to general youth activities, neighborhood surveillance, and the control of youth activities which often become overtures to far more serious crime and gang delinquency (Sampson, 1986).

The increase in one-adult households generally means that people in atomized conditions are deprived of protection and control. Families not only watch, but safeguard their own members, their property, and their neighborhood. A study of British estates found that, if the neighbors of lone parents are more likely to be victimized than the neighbors of two-parent households then, in turn, lone-parent households are more likely to be targets for crime (Sampson, 1987a). Similarly, research by Douglas Smith and Roger Jarjoura shows that the greater the percentage of lone parents with children in American neighborhoods, the higher the rates of crime and burglary in those neighborhoods (Smith and Jarjoura, 1988). Rates of family disruption are not the only factor. Population density, mobility, and the number of adolescents matter as well. What, by itself, did *not* seem to matter was the number of low-income families in a neighborhood. In turn, data from the National Longitudinal Survey of Youth found that, while young black men with lone mothers were twice as likely to engage in criminal activities compared with those raised by two parents, after holding constant variables like income, parental education, and residence, growing up in a neighborhood with high rates of family fragmentation tripled the possibility of this occurring (Hill and O'Neill, 1993).

If the number of unattached people in the community are, like the rates of family disruption, predictive of crime levels, then this is relevant to adult criminality as well. Robert Sampson (1987a) has shown how a city's divorce rate is a better predictor of the robbery rate than are measures of arrest and sentencing. Youth or adult, the individual with no family to vouch for him is likely to penetrate the criminal justice system further and for longer. As social disengagement is of a piece with family fragmentation, this militates against attempts to regenerate local communities or build cohesive neighborhoods. The same goes for the way that areas with high rates of family disruption tend to have low rates of participation in community politics, recreation, and educational activities. Lone mothers participate less than married women in social and educational organizations, and single men much less so than fathers. Communities with pronounced family disruption are likely to see a weakening of informal and voluntary organizations, many of which play crucial roles in linking youth to wider social institutions and fostering desirable principles and values (Sampson, 1987b).

If family life is generally stabilizing in the life of the neighborhood, then, in contrast to the much-worn feminist view of marriage as the enslaver of women, there is its greater and certainly more authentic role in the control of men. Single men are troublesome, and there is nothing new about the problem of disorderly young men. If they are disproportionately represented among the criminal and the riotous (Field and Southgate, 1982; Moens *et al.*, 1988), single and separated men are also far more likely to kill themselves, enter psychiatric care, take drugs, and drink too much (Dominian *et al.*, 1991).

The 'family man' role provides men with incentives for orderly and patient participation in the community as much as it provides discipline for children. Indeed, as David Blankenhorn (1995) has recently been at pains to point out, the concept of the family man has been largely inseparable from the definition of the *good man*. Traditionally, among British working-class people, marriage carried with it the right to be treated as adult and independent, and to be seen as socially adequate – or, not simply as a youth out for a good time, but rather, as a mature and responsible citizen (Simms and Smith, 1982, pp. 147–8). The family man role does not just compete for time with more self-centered and self-gratifying pursuits: people also behave differently when they recognize the claims of dependents and are concerned about their community. Instead of neighborhood standards being enforced by fathers, low marriage rates mean a decline of the responsible male and an increasing likelihood that men are not only going to be more inclined to opt out of social obligations, but become net contributors to the community's problems.

More subtle than offense statistics and welfare bills is the way that this may weaken general processes of care and education in society, where one generation exerts itself on behalf of another. Erik Erikson has spoken of *generativity,* and investigation has confirmed how men, in this case adoptive fathers, are generally far more likely to adopt positions in organizations, formal and informal, that involve the guidance and welfare of young people. Committed kinship thus builds other commitments. It is the foremost reservoir of altruistic social involvement, and shapes the moral capital of the next generation (Snarey *et al.*, 1987; Sundeen, 1990; Murray, 1994).

Moreover, without marriage not only are people deprived of a welcomed rite of passage into a desired and desirable status, but, in addition, society is deprived of its foremost corrective institution, or route out of lawbreaking, as so many investigations of recidivism will testify. In one study of persistent young offenders the respondents were asked what, besides the intimidating prospect of the adult courts and prisons, would help them reform themselves. The overwhelming response was 'that certain people might help' – Mums, Dads, sisters and girlfriends. 'I've got too much to lose,' said one respondent, who had a steady girlfriend (Hagell and Newburn, 1994). It should hardly surprise us that in the recent Home Office study, *Young People and Crime*, the variable most likely to exert an effect on male desistence was marriage, which increased the odds by a factor of three (Graham and Bowling, 1995; see also Sampson and Laub, 1993, for similar findings).

Marriage traditionally provided much of the explanation of why so many juvenile delinquents, even in the roughest areas, did so often grow out of misbehaving or 'drift out of delinquency'. While adventurous and expensive programs have continually sought that momentous change in the delinquent psyche which will send offenders forward transformed ever after, vast numbers of lawbreakers have been quietly 'rehabilitated' without benefit of, or even in spite of, treatment. David Matza has described how, as the gang boy grows up, his masculinity anxiety is 'somewhat reduced when someone becomes a man rather than a mere aspirant'. This is because, in the past anyway:

> Boys are less driven to prove manhood unconventionally through ... misdeeds when, with the passing of time, they may effortlessly exhibit the conventional signposts of manhood – physical appearance, the completion of school, job, marriage, and perhaps even children. (Matza, 1964, p. 55)

However, if marriage is the great gatekeeper to positive behavior, how can that 'drift out of delinquency', or process of spontaneous remission, occur when mothers are helped to manage independently of men and male self-esteem becomes detached from the status and satisfactory performance of the family man? Young males now, as investigations of desistance show, are having greater problems in acquiring the means for 'making a successful transition to adulthood'. They are less likely to 'enter into stable relationships with the opposite sex, form new families and eventually become economically independent, socially responsible and self-reliant individuals'. The result is that

> in effect, males are detached from the main institutions of social control for longer than females as they drift in and out of casual relationships and casual employment and attach themselves more permanently to groups of like-minded peers. (Graham and Bowling, 1995, pp. 94–5)

It may be that there are other roles through which men can make a direct contribution to the community. But endurable substitutes are not manufactured to order. There were once monastic institutions, but there is reason to doubt whether anything which managed to give a role to dispossessed men in the modern world would be necessarily benign. On the contrary, it has been argued forcefully elsewhere that as men's jobs in the old industries and manufactures go, taking with them the marriage tickets of unskilled and semi-skilled men, and the state increasingly supports the mother–child unit, we have reproduced the historic conditions for a warrior class. There is separation of economic activity from family maintenance, children reared apart from fathers, wealth subject to predation and male status determined by combat and sexual conquest, as young men deal in drugs and guns (Will, 1991). This is accompanied by the bifurcation of state domestic policy, with the 'simultaneous emergence of a police state to suppress the men and of a child care state to manage the children' (Gilder, 1973, p. 99). The complement of help for mothers to become 'self-sufficient' appears to be policing and prisons to control the male drones. That this has largely been the practical response to date can be seen in Britain's massive prison building program (including extra secure units for persistent young offenders).

While large numbers of men disconnected from the obligations, satisfactions, and membership of family life has historically been an abiding and pervasive fear for society, this momentous implication of lone parenthood has, as Geoff Dench (1993) alleges in his investigation of changing Afro-Caribbean family structure, long been avoided by commentators in Britain, and lone parents are still discussed almost entirely in terms of how the mothers cope. That there can be publications like *Crime and the Family*, from government-sponsored bodies and prominent research institutes, which completely ignore the impact of family breakdown on both adolescent control and the social involvement of men, defies reason (Utting *et al.*, 1993; Coote, 1994).

Otherwise, the matter tends to be brushed aside with the insistence that men should not need families, or employment prospects, to behave themselves. Anyway, why should women want anything to do with men as many are now? If this strategy deprives the child of close contact with half the human race, it also excludes half the human race from the means to transcend immediate self-interest. Nobody learns and upholds social rules from outside social relations and responsibilities, but only by being in the midst of these and maintaining them because they are their own. People have to live and teach the lesson, if they are to know and abide by it themselves.

It is difficult to see what public investment could offset the current deterioration of child well-being and social dislocation, following family fragmentation and the collapse of marriage. The eclipse of the institutions which sustain our moral environment is more than a problem at the level of socialization, or of social structure, with individuals isolated and estranged from the realities of family responsibilities and membership. In that the family is the primary moral domain, its rejection brings in tow the loss of those moral traditions that underpin basic social sympathy and identity, and serve to legitimize authority (Morgan, 1992). In their absence, law is simply a technique for controlling behavior; coercion necessarily becomes the only instrument available for the maintenance of minimal social control and individual submission depends upon cost–benefit analyses (Lasch, 1977). If we have to ask ourselves how the enforcement of regulations, not internal stability, can keep society from disorder, this brings home just how radical, and not only unprecedented, is the modern abandonment of the family.

REFERENCES

Bailey, W. C. (1971) Correctional outcome: An evaluation of one hundred reports. In L. Radzinowitz and M. E. Wolfgang (eds.), *Crime and Justice* 3 (pp. 187–94). New York: Basic Books.

Bebbington, A. and Miles, J. (1989) The background of children who enter local authority care. *British Journal of Social Work* 19, 349–68.

Blankenhorn, D. (1995) *Fatherless America*. New York: Basic Books.

Brody, S. R. (1976) *The Effectiveness of Sentencing – A Review of the Literature*. London: HMSO.

Bureau of Justice Statistics. (1988) *Survey of Youth in Custody*. Washington, DC: Department of Justice.

Cockett, M. and Tripp, J. (1994) *The Exeter Family Study: Family Breakdown and Its Impact on Children*. Exeter, England: University of Exeter Press.

Cornish, B. D. and Clarke, R. V. G. (1975) *Residential Treatment and Its Effects on Delinquency*. London: HMSO.

Coote, A. (ed.) (1994) *Families, Children and Crime*. London: Institute for Public Policy Research.

Coote, A., Harman, H. and Hewitt, P. (1990) *The Family Way*. London: Institute for Public Policy Research.

Council on Families in America. (1995) *Marriage in America: A Report to the Nation*. New York: Institute for American Values.

Dench, G. (1993) *From Extended Family to State Dependency*. Middlesex, England: Center for Community Studies, Middlesex University.

Dennis, N. and Erdos, G. (1992) *Families Without Fatherhood*. London: IEA Health and Welfare Unit.

Deschenes, E. P., Greenwood, P. W. and Adams, J. (1994) *An Evaluation of the Nokomis Challenge Program in Michigan*. Santa Monica, California: RAND.

Dominian, J., Mansfield, P., Dormor, D. and McAllister, F. (1991) *Marital Breakdown and the Health of the Nation*. London: One Plus One.

Dornbusch, S. M., *et al.* (1985) Single parents, extended households and the control of adolescents. *Child Development* 56, 326–41.

Essen, J., Lambert, L. and Head, J. (1976) School attainment of children who have been in care. *Child: Care, Health and Development* 2, 339–51.

Ferri, E. (1984) *Step Children: A National Study*. Windsor, England: NFER – Nelson Assessment Library.

Field, S. and Southgate, P. (1982) *Public Disorder: A Review of Research and a Study in One Inner City Area* (Study No. 72). London: HMSO.

Fortes, M. (1983) *Rules and the Emergence of Human Society* (Occasional Paper No. 39). London: Royal Society Anthropological Society.

Gilder, G. (1973) *Sexual Suicide*. New York: Quadrangle.

Glueck, S. and Glueck, E. (1950) *Unraveling Juvenile Delinquency*. Cambridge: Harvard University Press.

Gottfredson, M. R. and Hirschi, T. (1990) *A General Theory of Crime*. Stanford: Stanford University Press.

Graham, J. and Bowling, B. (1995) *Young People and Crime* (Home Office Research Study No. 145). London: HMSO.

Greenberg, D. F. (ed.) (1977) The correctional effects of correction: A survey of evaluations. In *Corrections and Punishment* (pp. 111–48). Beverly Hills, California: Sage Publications.

Greenwood, P. W., Deschenes, E. P. and Adams, J. (1993) *Chronic Juvenile Offenders: Final Results from the Skillman Aftercare Experiment*. Santa Monica, California: RAND.

Greenwood, P. W. and Turner, S. (1993) *Evaluation of the Paint Creek Youth Center: A Residential Program for Serious Delinquents*. Santa Monica, California: RAND.

Hagell, A. and Newburn, T. (1994) *Persistent Young Offenders*. London: Policy Studies Institute.

Hill, M. A. and O'Neill, J. (1993) *Underclass Behaviors in the United States: Measurement and Analysis of Determinants*. New York: City University of New York, Baruch College.

Hirschi, T. (1983) Crime and the family. In J. Q. Wilson and J. Petersilia (eds.), *Crime and Public Policy* (pp. 53–68). San Francisco: Institute for Contemporary Studies.

——. (1995) The Family. In J. Q. Wilson and J. Petersilia (eds.), *Crime*. San Francisco: Institute for Contemporary Studies.

Home Office, Research and Statistics Department (1991) *National Prison Survey Research Study* (No. 128). London: HMSO.

Lasch, C. (1977) *Haven in a Heartless World.* New York: Basic Books.

Lipton, D., Martinson, R. and Wilks, J. (1975) *The Effectiveness of Correctional Treatment: A Survey of Evaluation Studies.* New York: Praeger.

Marsh, P. (1987) Social work and fathers – an exclusive practice? In C. Lewis and M. O'Brien (eds.), *Reassessing Fatherhood.* Thousand Oaks, California: Sage.

Martin, B. (1981) *A Sociology of Contemporary Cultural Change.* Oxford: Basil Blackwell.

Martinson, R. (1974) What works? Questions and answers about prison reform. *The Public Interest* (Spring), 22–54.

Matsueda, R. L. and Heimer, K. (1987) Race, family structure, and delinquency: A test of differential association and social control theories. *American Sociological Review* 52, 826–40.

Matza, David. (1964) *Delinquency and Drift.* Chichester: John Wiley & Sons.

McLanahan, S. (1988) The consequences of single parenthood for subsequent generations. *Focus.* Institute for Research on Poverty, University of Wisconsin-Madison.

Moens, F. G. G., Haenen, W. and Van de Voorde, H. (1988) Epidemiological aspects of suicide among the young in selected European countries. *Journal of Epidemiology and Community Health* 42, 279–85.

Morgan, P. (1978) *Delinquent Fantasies.* London: Temple Smith.

——. (1992) Fidelity. In D. Anderson (ed.), *The Loss of Virtue.* London: Social Affairs Unit/National Review Book.

Murray, D. W. (1994) Poor suffering bastards: An anthropologist looks at illegitimacy. *Policy Review* 68, 9–15.

Newson, E., Newson, J. and Lewis, C. (1982) Father participation through childhood and its relationship with career aspirations and delinquency. In N. Beail and J. McGuire (eds.), *Fathers: Psychological Perspectives.* New York: Junction Books.

Riley, D. and Shaw, M. (1985) *Parental Supervision and Juvenile Delinquency.* London: Home Office Research Study, No. 83.

Rutter, M. and Smith, D. J. (1995) *Psychosocial Disorders in Young People.* London: John Wiley & Sons.

Sacks, J. (1995) *Faith in the Future.* London: Darton, Longman and Todd.

Sampson, R. J. (1986) Crime in the cities: The effects of formal and informal social control. In A. J. Reiss, Jr. and M. Tonry (eds.), *Communities and Crime, Crime and Justice* 8 (pp. 271–312). Chicago: University of Chicago Press.

——. (1987a) Does an intact family reduce burglary risks for neighbors? *Sociology and Social Research* 71, 404–7.

——. (1987b) Urban black violence: The effect of male joblessness and family disruption. *American Journal of Sociology* 93, 348–82.

Sampson, R. J. and Laub, J. H. (1993) *Crime in the Making: Pathways and Turning Points Through Life.* Cambridge: Harvard University Press.

Simms, M. and Smith, C. (1982) Young fathers: Attitudes to marriage and family life. In Lorna McKee and Margaret O'Brien (eds.), *The Father Figure.* London: Tavistock.

Smith, D. and Jarjoura, G. R. (1988) Social structure and criminal victimization. *Journal of Research in Crime and Delinquency* 25, 27–52.

Snarey, J., *et al.* (1987) The role of parenting in men's psychosocial development: A longitudinal study of early adulthood infertility and midlife generativity. *Generational Psychology* 23, 593–603.

Sundeen, R. A. (1990) Family life course status and volunteer behavior. *Sociological Perspectives* 33, 483–500.

Suttles, G. (1968) *The Social Order of the Slum: Ethnicity and Territory in the Inner City*. Chicago: University of Chicago Press.

Utting, D., Bright, B. and Henricson, C. (1993) *Crime and the Family* (Occasional Paper No. 16). London: Family Policy Studies Center.

Wadsworth, M. (1979) *The Roots of Delinquency*. New York: Martin Robertson.

Wallerstein, J. S. and Blakeslee, S. (1989) *Second Chances*. New York: Ticknor and Fields.

Wallerstein, J. S. and Kelly, J. B. (1980) *Surviving the Breakup*. New York: Basic Books.

West, D. J. (1982) *Delinquency: Its Roots, Careers and Prospects*. London: Heinemann.

Wilkins, L. T. (1969) *Evaluation of Penal Measures*. New York: Random House.

Will, G. F. (1991) Nature and the Male Sex. *Newsweek* (7 June).

Wilson, J. Q. (1983) *Thinking about Crime* (2nd ed.). New York: Basic Books.

9 Reducing Delinquency by Improving Character
Jinney S. Smith

INTRODUCTION

In both the United States and Great Britain, there is today a high level of concern about the moral state of society generally and of young people especially. In Great Britain, a 1995 news article headline in *The Sunday Times* about the increasing rate of violent crime among 10- to 13-year-old males declared, 'The "savage generation" hits Britain'. In a 1995 news article about the 160 per cent increase in the number of murders committed by teenagers since 1985 in the United States, a commentator declared, 'What is particularly alarming ... is the absence of any morality among the younger generation which allows children as young as ten to commit murder without feeling any sense of wrong'. Furthermore, the growing juvenile delinquency problems experienced in America has led to heightened concerns about the values of not only children and teenagers, but of society generally. A summer 1994 *Newsweek* poll found that 76 per cent of Americans believe their country is in a 'moral and spiritual decline'. The same can be said for Britain, where *The Guardian* in October 1996 described how 'the Conservatives, Labour and Liberal Democrats began a stampede yesterday to claim they were closest to the moral agenda for the regeneration of Britain', proposed by the widow of a murdered teacher, to curb juvenile violence.

In recent years, in both the US and UK, reforms have been undertaken to improve the morals, or character, of young people. In response to the stabbing death of a schoolteacher which galvanized public opinion, the British government in October 1996 announced the creation of good citizenship awards for children to promote moral behavior and civic values. Earlier, in 1994, the British government revamped the national school curriculum to include moral education, and provided teaching aids based on Lawrence Kohlberg's theory of moral development. The manuals instruct teachers about the importance of eliciting from students the reasons for their opinions and describe the progression of stages, or 'focus of concern' (ranging from self to wider society), which they should notice in students.

In the United States, where education is under local government control, reform has been piecemeal but there is undoubtedly a clear trend towards greater devotion of class time to character education. In 1997 a national consortium comprised of 40 public and private organizations was created to spearhead the burgeoning character education movement:

> Character education, civil education, service learning, learning to serve – the various ideas loosely tied together in the group's mission have slowly grown in influence in recent years. Many states and school systems already use such programs, although on a scattered basis. The idea of the partnership is to bring them to the center of the nation's educational mission. (Applebome, 1997, p. A12)

What underlies the popularity of these educational reforms is the promise of reduced delinquency. Most notably, evaluations of such programs focus on the improvements in students' attitudes and behavior achieved. In the UK, the crime-fighting purpose of moral education was made explicit by the address to which teachers could write to order moral education materials: 'Crack Crime, PO Box 999'. To reinforce this purpose – to affect the behavior of children – the materials state that,

> During the trialling of this material, it was noted that the atmosphere of several classes which had a citizenship session roughly once a week, had noticeably improved in terms of the children's attitudes towards each other and towards mature respectful discussion. (Rowe and Newton, 1994, p. 7)

In the United States there is also much experimentation going on with values and moral education materials, also with the aim of addressing the larger juvenile delinquency crisis. One difference between the US and UK, however, is that, in the US, such educational programs are rarely called 'moral education', but rather 'character' or 'civic' education, or, in some cases, 'anti-violence'. As Kuhmerker (1973) observed, 'Moral education is a term that is seldom used in the United States. ... [I]n the minds of many adults the term is so closely tied to religious indoctrination, that we use a variety of substitute terms to avoid the controversy' (p. 359).

One example of a typical character education program is that of the Jefferson Center for Character Education, based in California, one of dozens of such centers located across the US. Its widely implemented character education program is called STAR, which is an acronym for both the goal of the program (Success Through Accepting Responsibility) and the general lesson of the curriculum (to Stop, Think, Act, and Review). According to their promotional literature, about 4500 schools in the US have used the Jefferson STAR materials with over 1.5 million students. The Jefferson Center commissioned California Survey Research to conduct an evaluation of the efficacy of the program in reducing school misbehavior and enhancing the academic achievement of student participants. Based on interviews with teachers and administrators at 25 Los Angeles elementary and junior high schools who had used the materials, the study found that the following results were achieved between the time the use of the materials began in the fall of 1990 and the time of the study in the spring of 1991: major discipline problems (such as fighting) fell by 25 per cent, minor discipline problems fell by 39 per cent, and tardy students sent to the office per month fell by 40 per cent. The absolute numbers, however, were small (for example, major disciplinary problems fell from 20 per month in the fall of 1990 to 15 per month in the spring of 1991). None the less, the percentages figure prominently in the Jefferson Center's promotional brochure.

These examples of trying to fight delinquency through revamped educational curriculums are largely preventative in nature. The literature on the efficacy of such delinquency prevention approaches is small and largely anecdotal, primarily because of the scattered nature and recent appearance of such reforms in the US and UK respectively. However, what research does exist shows such programs are promising and, at worst, certainly do not harm students, with the exception of the opportunity cost of lost class time which could have been devoted to other subjects. On the other hand, much more research exists on the rehabilitative use of moral or character education programs: that is, the ability of such programs to rehabilitate identified juvenile delinquents. It is this body of research that is the focus of this chapter.

Tracing the causes of delinquency to some type of character deficiency has been both the inspiration of academic research and the cornerstone of popular opinion about delinquency's root causes. However, the widespread belief that juvenile delinquents are morally defective (or outright amoral), and that such moral deficits lay at the heart of delinquency, should not imply that everyone has the same thing in mind when discussing 'moral reasoning'. In fact, what is meant by 'moral reasoning' in the popular sense overlaps only partly with how it has been studied, primarily in the field of psychology. Nevertheless, it is this academic base of research upon which public policy is being constructed. Roy Feldman, for example, criticizes Lawrence Kohlberg and his supporters for capturing popular attention with claims of increasing moral reasoning when, in fact, 'Kohlberg and his colleagues have a restricted, technical, operational meaning: a positive change in score on Kohlberg's Moral Judgment Interview, an instrument that scales the subject's verbally stated reasons for endorsing hypothetical courses of action' (Feldman, 1980, p. 288). In addition, Locke (1983) emphasizes the importance of moral content over a Kohlbergian type of moral reasoning ability, arguing that enhancing moral reasoning has not been proven conclusively to improve behavior. Before the evidence of the rehabilitative powers of moral education can be discussed, then, this discrepancy between popular and academic conceptions of moral reasoning necessitates an introduction to the major thinkers, theories, and methodologies involved in assessing and altering individual moral reasoning.

HISTORICAL AND THEORETICAL DEVELOPMENT OF MORAL REASONING THEORIES

Jean Piaget, the Swiss psychologist (1896–1980), was the first to outline systematically the development of children's understanding of the origins and purposes of rules in his 1932 work, *The Moral Judgment of the Child* (for a discussion of Piaget and Kohlberg, see Duska and Whelan, 1975). Piaget found that from ages 2 to 8, children view rules laid down by adults as sacred, and all they know about rules is that they must be obeyed. An illustration of the seriousness with which young children view rules is provided by the following account: 'One group of researchers asked some primary school children what are the worst crimes anyone can commit and received the answer that the worst crime of all is killing people and the second most serious is running in the corridor' (Smith, 1978, p. 59). This is what Piaget called the stage of 'heteronomy'. Beginning around ages 7 and 8, children enter the stage of 'autonomy', when they begin to understand the purpose and origin of rules, and no longer view the rules of adults as inherently sacred. The critical activity that brings about this transformation is 'cooperative play' with other children – playing games in which rules are agreed to and followed for the benefit of all. This is how children begin to internalize the value of following rules.

Against the backdrop of this developmental explanation of how children understand and practice rules, Piaget conducted additional research into how children define lying and how they ascribe blame. Up until age 5, children define all lies as simply naughty words. During the transitional period of ages 5 through 8, lies are conceptualized mistakes or statements that are not true (such as tall tales). Between ages 8 to 10, children begin distinguishing mistakes from lies, and it is not until around age 10 that children label only intentionally false statements as lies. Another change, regarding how children ascribe blame to actors, also begins around age 8 when children begin to consider intent in assessing the blameworthiness of an act; before this time, children typically only consider the extent of the tangible or quantifiable results of an act. For example, if told about two girls who broke some cups, children under age 8 typically ascribe more blame to a child who broke ten cups while trying to help her mother, whereas older children ascribe more blame to the child who broke only one on purpose.

Building on the work of Piaget's stages of heteronomy and autonomy, Lawrence Kohlberg (1927–987), who was professor of education and social psychology at Harvard University, began publishing his theory of cognitive stages in the late 1960s. It was his longitudinal study of the development of 50 male subjects that shaped the formulation of his theory of moral stages. His study subjects, ranging in age from 10 to 28 at the beginning of the study, were followed up every 3 years for 18 years, at which time they were administered moral reasoning tests. The developmental progress in moral reasoning, in terms of how the subjects evaluated dilemmas, was found to show four stable characteristics: (1) invariant stage development; (2) that subjects comprehend the reasoning of only one stage beyond their own; (3) that subjects are attracted to the logic of the first stage above their own; and finally, (4) that 'cognitive disequilibrium', which simply means being confronted with views challenging your own, is necessary for stage progression.

In developing his theory, which is based on a justice orientation, Kohlberg's philosophical influences included social contract theory, or Utilitarianism (exemplified by Jeremy Bentham's 'the greatest happiness of the greatest number' principle as well as John Stuart Mill's contention that each person's happiness is equally important), and Kantian ethics, including the categorical imperative as well as the notion that one should always treat others as an end unto themselves and never as a means (Crittenden, 1990).

Kohlberg's theory initially included six stages of moral development. Stages one and two, the 'pre-conventional stages', are found primarily among children under the age of 9. At these stages decision-making is driven by the desires to seek pleasure and avoid pain. The pre-conventional stages correspond roughly to Piaget's stage of heteronomy. Stages three and four are the 'conventional' stages, representing the dominant stages for adolescents and adults. The key prerequisites to thinking conventionally are developing empathy and recognizing the value and necessity of conforming to the rules and values of the larger group or social order (Kohlberg, 1976).

The 'post-conventional' or 'principled' stages, five and six, are not commonly found even among adults, and are reserved for those who, even though they may act on and uphold the same rules as conventional thinkers do, can enunciate reasons for their views that are based on their group's consensus or their own morality after critical reflection. Stage five, with its emphasis on individual rights and rule of law, has been called the 'official morality' of the United States Constitution. Sixth-stage thinking, because it was not empirically supported by Kohlberg's or other's research, has been discontinued as a theoretical category. Kohlberg's stages were not intended to assess the actual behavior of subjects, but instead to reveal how subjects evaluate moral dilemmas and competing claims for justice: 'moral behavior is not a proper external criterion for "validating" a moral judgment test' (Kohlberg, 1976, p. 46). Thus, in addition to failing to appear regularly, the sixth stage caused additional problems, because to illustrate such moral reasoning Kohlberg often needed to resort to the statements and *actions* of martyrs such as Martin Luther King, Jr., or Mahatma Gandhi (Duska and Whelan, 1975).

The moral reasoning tests used to assign subjects to one of these five stages (also called global stage scores) or a moral maturity score (ranging correspondingly from 100 to 500 points for more precise measurement) are derived from open-ended responses to moral dilemmas. A subject's major stage is the stage reflected by at least 50 per cent of all responses; a minor stage is assigned if at least 25 per cent of all responses reflect an additional single stage. Subjects' responses to examiners' questions about why they believe a certain resolution to a dilemma is good or bad are scored by comparing them to prototype or model responses for each stage. There are no right or wrong answers *per se* – only more or less principled reasons for approving or disapproving a course of action.

Although there is no standard moral reasoning test, the tests typically comprise of several dilemma stories, often culled from the numerous volumes Kohlberg and his colleagues have published containing model dilemmas and scoring guides. The following example illustrates the application of such tests. One of the most commonly used moral dilemmas is the 'Heinz dilemma', a story about a husband who steals an expensive medicine for his dying wife after all legal attempts to obtain it have failed. In response to the question, 'Was Heinz right or wrong?', for example, a pre-conventional (or stage two) response would be that he was right to steal the drug because the alternative would be that his wife would die and he would have to pay for a costly funeral (a response which actually turned up in one study). If the respondent said the husband was right, because otherwise his family and friends would be disappointed that he didn't help his wife, that response would be scored at stage three. However, if the subject said that the husband was wrong because all thefts are inexcusable and law and order must be maintained, that response would be scored at stage four. A stage five response would be that the husband was wrong because society had decided that it was important to allow high profits in medical sales so that medical research would be encouraged for the benefit of all sick people. Finally, if it still existed, a typical stage six response would be that the husband did the right thing, because, although one should respect the property of others, there is a higher moral law and a universal principle of justice at work which demands respect for each person's life, and therefore makes the written law which allows such an injustice illegitimate.

One of the most striking features of the more principled justifications is the 'sheer cognitive power obviously required' to produce them (Lickona, 1976). This is a common critique of Kohlberg's theory and testing method, because performance on moral reasoning tests has generally been found to be highly correlated with IQ-test performance, and the contribution of high IQ to reasoning at the higher post-conventional moral stages has been described by Kohlberg as a 'necessary but not sufficient condition' (Lickona, 1976). In terms of testing delinquents this is especially troublesome, because, as Jurkovic and others have argued, 'The deficiencies of many delinquents in moral judgment may be a direct function of poor verbal-referential abilities, a weakness in this group that has been well documented' (1980, p. 723; see also Arbuthnot and Gordon, 1987).

One solution to this problem was the creation of the Defining Issues Test (DIT), created by J. R. Rest and his colleagues in the early 1970s (for this discussion, see Schlaefli, Rest and Thoma, 1985; Smetana, 1990). The DIT sought to compensate for the very high verbal abilities required by Kohlberg's open-ended dilemma interviews by providing subjects with a list which contained a variety of reasons representing each of the stages.

Subjects read the list, then choose statements from it that represent their own reasoning. Based on the number of 'post-conventional' or 'principled' items selected, the 'P-index', ranging in value from zero to 95, can be calculated. The DIT is essentially a recognition test, and accordingly subjects generally score higher on it than they would on a Kohlberg-style test. For example, stage five scores are relatively rare among adults taking the traditional moral reasoning test; however, even adolescents often agree with some stage five reasons presented on the DIT, thereby elevating their scores. (In one sense, such results support Kohlberg's theory, since he theorized that people are attracted to higher-stage reasoning.)

Another critique has to do with the universality of Kohlberg's moral reasoning stages. However, Snarey's (1985) review of 45 studies in 27 different cultural areas (ranging from the Bahamas to India to Turkey) generally supports Kohlberg's claims that his theory is universally applicable across cultures. Another, more contentious debate over Kohlberg's theory of moral development and scoring methodology is grounded in feminist critique. Carol Gilligan's 1982 book, *In a Different Voice*, argued that females score lower than males on Kohlberg-based moral reasoning tests because women base moral decisions on a care orientation, rather than the justice orientation more common to men. Kohlberg himself had called stage three a 'functional morality for housewives and mothers but not for professionals and businessmen' (Crittendon, 1990, p. 88). Furthermore, Gilligan argues that the overwhelming justice orientation of stages four and beyond makes Kohlberg's test inappropriate to use with female subjects because it penalizes their instinctive caring orientation and results in women having lower scores, on average, than men (Crittendon, 1990). Although research findings have generally rejected Gilligan's criticisms, there have been a handful of supportive findings, thus fueling the debate (see Baumrind, 1986; Friedman *et al.*, 1987; Krebs *et al.*, 1994; Walker, 1984; and Walker, 1986). However, even those who reject Gilligan's claims have praised her contribution to the literature. Colby and Damon (1983), while denying Gilligan's claims that males and females reason differently and that Kohlberg's moral reasoning tests are biased against females, still credit Gilligan with introducing a new methodology to moral reasoning research (using real-world decision-making) as well as bringing attention to 'care' aspects of moral reasoning.

REVIEW OF RESEARCH ON JUVENILE DELINQUENTS

The body of research on the moral reasoning of juvenile delinquents can be divided into three types. (Such research has also been carried out on adult offenders, and findings from that literature are comparable to the juvenile delinquent literature reviewed below.)

The first type of research has been concerned with establishing whether or not delinquents reason differently than non-delinquents. On this point, the research has found that delinquents, compared to their non-delinquent peers, generally (though not always) achieve lower moral reasoning scores. Adolescent delinquents generally achieve pre-conventional, or stage one or two, scores, whereas their non-delinquent peers achieve conventional, or stage three or four, scores (Arbuthnot, 1984; Arbuthnot and Gordon, 1987; Chandler and Moran, 1990; Henggeler, 1989; Lee and Prentice, 1978; Nelson *et al.*, 1990; Raine, 1993; and Smetana, 1990).

There are a few caveats about this general finding, however. The typical research protocol for these studies often involves administering a moral reasoning test, the vast majority of which use either the traditional Kohlberg-type test or the DIT, to a group of identified delinquents and a control group matched on a few key variables. Often, the juvenile delinquents selected for study are institutionalized, and this research has been criticized for relying too heavily on the captive audience of institutionalized delinquents. This is especially problematic because studies in which delinquents are identified through self-reporting generally find that there are no differences between them and their non-delinquent peers (Raine, 1993; Thornton, 1987). This finding, furthermore, may be explained by institutionalization itself. Kohlberg recognized the role of negative environments (such as those lacking role-taking opportunities which foster empathy) on moral development, and argued that 'monolithic or homogeneous lower-stage environments', such as orphanages and prisons, inhibit or reverse the moral development of their inhabitants (Kohlberg, 1976, p. 51). And, finally, there is the most fundamental challenge to this entire line of inquiry: Is this the correct way to measure moral reasoning?

The second type of research involves attempts to raise the moral reasoning stages of delinquents to the conventional level through an intervention called the moral discussion group. The moral discussion group, during which members are subject to 'cognitive disequilibrium' by facing challenges to their own immature moral reasoning from more mature group members or leaders, capitalizes on the attraction people are supposed to have to the reasoning of the first stage beyond their own. Also, to ensure that it is the moral discussion group that is responsible for the change, these studies usually include a control group, and sometimes even include an additional experimental group whose members participate in some type of common, therapeutic activity (such as group meetings). The success of such interventions in actually raising the moral reasoning of delinquents has been mixed, and, more importantly, methodologically difficult to establish (Jurkovic, 1980). To begin with, the changes tend to be small – usually between one-fifth and one-half of a stage (see Arbuthnot, 1984; Fleetwood and Parish, 1976; Gardner, 1983; Gibbs *et al.*, 1984; Niles, 1986; and Rosenkoetter *et al.*, 1980). However, such results are *prima facie* impressive when considering that the interventions credited for bringing them about are often neither long in duration nor intensive (for example, two hours a week for five weeks is a typical arrangement).

The second problem has to do with methods for scoring the traditional Kohlberg test, which is more popular than the objective DIT test. It requires significant training to be able to score competently the responses given to open-ended dilemmas. Even for the well-trained, however, the high subjectivity of the test causes problems:

> Expert scorers ... scored 20 protocols coded to disguise all identification of person and time. Ten protocols were randomly selected from the pool of Form A interviews from this project

and ten Form B interviews from the same source. The mean intercoder difference [disagreement between two coders] in Moral Maturity Score (MMS) points was 14.5 for Form A, 20.4 for Form B, and 17.45 (*S.D.* = *13.7*) for the two forms combined. ... Intracoder reliability (score/rescore) was computed by having the [same] scorer rescore 15 protocols at an interval of two weeks. An average discrepancy of 23 MMS points was found between the original and rescore of the same protocol. (Feldman, 1980, p. 324)

Keeping in mind that the average increase in moral reasoning stage achieved by successful interventions is only about one-fifth to one-half a stage (or between 20 and 50 points), the difficulty becomes obvious.

The final type of research on juvenile delinquency and moral reasoning has to do with the relationship between moral reasoning and behavior. The fact that there are interventions carried out to raise the moral reasoning of delinquents indicates that some believe there is a positive relationship between moral reasoning and behavior; otherwise, why else would one bother?

In 1980, Augusto Blasi published an exhaustive review of this question, examining 'behavior' in a variety of domains, and reached the very tentative conclusion that the following hypothesis was supported: Moral reasoning, as measured by the DIT and Kohlberg's test, is positively related to what can be called 'good' behavior. Of twelve studies which examined the relationship between moral reasoning and 'real life behavior' (such as classroom behavior and sexual promiscuity), six supported, three rejected, and three were mixed on the above hypothesis. Of seventeen studies that examined the relationship between moral reasoning and honesty, seven supported, seven rejected, and three showed mixed results on the hypothesis. This is not surprising, since it complements Hartshorne and May's large body of research into character, comprising several experiments involving over 11 000 children during the 1920s and 1930s. The results led to the formation of their 'doctrine of specificity' – that honesty is highly situation-dependent – which was confirmed by the very low correlation between lying, cheating, and stealing behaviors

(Burton, 1976; Lickona, 1976). Interestingly, one study found that in a sample of college students and prisoners, although 17 per cent of the prisoners cheated on a test compared to 10 per cent of the college students, 34 per cent of the prisoners who cheated, versus 12 per cent of the college students, confessed (Burton, 1976). Finally, Blasi (1980) reviewed 19 studies which examined the relationship between moral reasoning and altruistic behavior, and found that 11 strongly supported the hypothesis.

One study evaluated the effect that participating in a moral discussion group had not only on moral reasoning, but also on future delinquency. Prentice's (1972) study found that a group of delinquents exposed to a moral reasoning intervention showed average improvement on a post-test when compared to control subjects; however, a 9-month follow-up showed that there were no differences in the number or type of offenses committed by the two groups. In another study, Feldman (1980) reviewed a Kohlberg intervention set in an adult prison. Kohlberg developed models for Just Community schools and prisons, based on the principles of participatory democracy, justice and fairness, and moral discussion. However, they were not practiced strictly according to the ideal; the subordinate nature of inmates and children to prison and school administrators was never in doubt, even in one-man, one-vote systems, although the overall 'social climate' was perceived more favorably by Just Community participants (Feldman, 1980). In the end, Feldman concluded that 'the relationship between the programs promoted by Kohlberg and his associates and Kohlberg's theory is ambiguous. Evidence available indicates no significant moral growth and no rehabilitation of prison inmates in comparison with the alternative programs examined' (1980, p. 315). Still, 'interviews with Just Community female inmates elicited frequent statements that a benefit of moral development is that they will be less likely to be reincarcerated after graduating from the Just Community' (p. 309, footnote).

A final issue is what can a moral reasoning perspective tell us about the differences in offending between males and females. Females in Britain make up 20 per cent of all known young offenders, and compared to males, female delinquents commit proportionately more theft (Worrall, 1995). Roughly the same is true in the United States. Furthermore, girls are more likely than boys to be found guilty of what Smetana (1990) calls 'conventional offenses' (or status offenses, such as truancy or sexual promiscuity). Because, as already noted, this body of research draws heavily on institutionalized delinquents, and female delinquents are relatively rare in such settings, very little research has explored the moral reasoning of female delinquents. Of the five studies Smetana reviewed in her 1990 article, two found no sex differences, while the other three 'reported some evidence consistent with the hypothesis that female delinquents may be at developmentally higher levels of moral maturity than males' (p. 171).

CONCLUSION

A review of the literature about the moral reasoning of juvenile delinquents raises as many questions as it answers. Despite the number of studies conducted, no clear consensus emerges, although results tend to be more positive than negative. One reason for this is because there are several shortcomings in the current methodologies used. More rigorous studies that avoid the pitfalls of the current literature must be conducted. The second reason why more study is needed is that, despite the shortcomings of the research, the public's overwhelming belief in the causal force of moral deficits in producing delinquency is rapidly transforming not only education policy, but also juvenile justice programming. In Great Britain, the Citizenship Foundation developed in 1993 a set of materials called 'Us and Them: A thinking skills program for offenders', which is intended for use by juvenile offenders in secure settings to improve moral reasoning. As of 1995, the program had been tested successfully, and nationwide implementation is now under way. In the United States, at the state and local levels, experimentation with character training in justice settings is also growing, and is taking a variety of forms, such as moral discussion groups and fatherhood training for young delinquent males (Laub *et al.*, 1995).

   In addition to explicit character or values training, there is another type of program which provides a sort of moral education for offenders: victim–offender mediation. Given the structure and content of such meetings, in which offenders come face to face with either their own or others' victims and have their own reasoning and past behavior challenged, mediation should be classified as a type of moral education for offenders. Although victim–offender mediation has existed for several years, such programs are becoming more popular in light of the victim's rights movements in the US and UK. Furthermore, they appear to benefit both victims and offenders. One study of 26 victim–offender mediations held in 1984 in Rochester, England, found that in addition to helping the victims overcome their traumatic experiences, the exercise left convicted burglars feeling much more sympathy for burglary victims and more aware of how their offending harms others (Launay, 1987). Going into the mediation, the offenders reported expecting that the main concern of the victims would be financial, and, anticipating this, many offenders gave advice on how to avoid future victimization. After the mediation, offenders expressed surprise at the psychological trauma experienced by victims. Furthermore, a control group was employed in this study, in which offenders met with victim support volunteers rather than actual victims. The attitudes of offenders who were in the control group changed very little after the exercise, indicating that there is something about confronting victims which effects changes in the thinking of offenders. However, while there is anecdotal evidence that offenders who participate in a mediation have lower recidivism rates than those who do not, more systematic research is also needed in this area.

Finally, any discussion about improving children's character would be incomplete without mentioning the role of parents as moral educators. The literature overwhelmingly indicates that juvenile delinquency is rooted in the early family life of children, and primarily in the parent–child relationship. In their analysis of over 50 studies (dating from 1940 to 1985) which examined the relationship between childhood behavior and later delinquency, Stouthamer-Loeber and Loeber (1988) found 'strong consensus about many factors predictive of later delinquency' (p. 345). The following factors were most predictive of delinquent outcomes: child variables (aggression, drug use, truancy, lying, stealing, low educational attainment) and family variables (poor supervision, parental neglect, parental lack of involvement, rejection of the child, and parental absence).

In a much earlier study, Glueck (1966) constructed a delinquency prediction table that incorporated 'under-the-roof climate of the home' factors based on empirical testing to identify potential delinquents by age 17 at 2 to 3 years of age (p. 6). The five factors included in the prediction table were the pathology of the parents, parent–child attachment, childhood restlessness, childhood destructiveness, and child defiance to parental authority. Based on a sample of 873 male subjects, 89 per cent of those predicted to be non-delinquent were non-delinquent while 90 per cent of those predicted to be delinquent were in fact delinquent, yielding a false positive rate of 10 per cent. Glueck (1966) developed another prediction table, tested on 984 subjects and designed to predict potential delinquents by age 17 at 5 to 6 years of age. Only three factors were included in this prediction table: ratings of maternal supervision, maternal discipline, and family cohesiveness. The table correctly predicted 91 per cent of non-delinquents and 89 per cent of delinquents, again yielding a relatively low 11 per cent false positive rate. More recent studies by Farrington (1989), whose sample consisted by over 400 English boys followed longitudinally, and Sampson and Laub (1993), who reanalyzed the Glueck sample of 1000 Boston boys followed longitudinally, reinforce previous findings that good parenting is critical to preventing delinquency.

We know that parent–child relationships characterized by neglect, weak bonds, low nurturing, and abuse result in higher rates of subsequent delinquency and criminality, among a host of other maladaptive outcomes. Additionally, children who are weakly attached to school or perform poorly in school also are more likely to engage in delinquency and subsequent adult criminality. On the other hand, despite severe environmental stresses such as poverty, children who are attached to competent and nurturing parents and school show remarkable resilience in avoiding such maladaptive adult outcomes. These research findings are complemented by public opinion as well. In a 1995 nationwide Gallup Poll, American respondents reported that the number one cause of youth violence was lack of parental control and poor discipline in the home (Maguire and Pastore, 1996, p. 131). In light of this consensus, both the British and American public are turning to improving parenting as a means to fight delinquency, and programs which provide extensive social support services and training to families at risk of poor parenting are being implemented and have been found to be successful (Schorr, 1988). In addition, many hospitals increasingly provide parenting classes to new parents. One of the more fundamental changes which has been recommended is to begin mandatory parenting classes in all high schools (Leitenberg, 1987).

Turning to moral education as a means to fight delinquency is hardly a new idea. As Hersh, Miller and Fielding (1980) point out, in the United States the system of free public education was developed early in the nineteenth century as 'the ultimate bulwark against crime, revolution and degeneracy' (p. 17; see also Kaestle, 1984). Moral education, then intricately tied up with religious education in a way unthinkable today, was integrated into every facet of education. In 1808, the widely used *Boston Primer* taught the alphabet through rhyming couplets such as 'In Adam's fall, we sinned all', to instill religious doctrine and teach the letter 'a', or 'The idle fool is whipt (*sic*) at school' to instill discipline and teach the letter 'f'. Even though the means being used today to improve the character of youth are drastically different from those used in the past, the goal and motivation are essentially unchanged: to raise good citizens who will respect the law and behave well amidst a widespread perception that civil society itself is under attack.

REFERENCES

Applebome, P. (1997) Plan adds 'civil education' to the basics of schooling. *The New York Times* (14 April), A12.

Arbuthnot, J. (1984) Moral reasoning development programs in prison: Cognitive-developmental and critical reasoning approaches. *Journal of Moral Education* 13, 112–23.

Arbuthnot, J. and Gordon, D. (1987) Personality. In H. C. Quay (ed.), *Handbook of Juvenile Delinquency* (pp. 139–83). New York: John Wiley & Sons.

Baumrind, D. (1986) Sex differences in moral reasoning: Response to Walker's (1984) conclusion that there are none. *Child Development* 57, 511–21.

Blasi, A. (1980) Bridging moral cognition and moral action: A critical review of the literature. *Psychological Bulletin* 88, 1–45.

Burton, R. (1976) Honesty and dishonesty. In T. Lickona (ed.), *Moral Development and Behavior: Theory, Research, and Social Issues* (pp. 173–97). New York: Holt, Rinehart and Winston.

Chandler, M. and Moran, T. (1990) Psychopath and moral development: A comparative study of delinquent and nondelinquent youth. *Development and Psychopathology* 2, 227–46.

Colby, A. and Damon, W. (1983) Listening to a different voice: A review of Gilligan's *In a Different Voice. Merrill-Palmer Quarterly* 29, 473–81.

Crittenden, P. (1990) *Learning to be Moral: Philosophical Thoughts about Moral Development*. Atlantic Heights, New Jersey: Humanities Press International.

Duska, R. and Whelan, M. (1975) *Moral Development: A Guide to Piaget and Kohlberg*. New York State: Missionary Society of St. Paul the Apostle.

Farrington, D. P. (1989) Later adult outcomes of offenders and nonoffenders. In M. Brambring, F. Losel and H. Skowronek (eds.), *Children At Risk: Assessment, Longitudinal Research and Intervention* (pp. 220–44). New York: Walter de Gruyter.

Feldman, R. E. (1980) The promotion of moral development in prisons and schools. In R. W. Wilson and G. J. Schochet (eds.), *Moral Development and Politics* (pp. 286–328). New York: Praeger.

Fleetwood, R. and Parish, T. (1976) Relationship between moral development test scores of juvenile delinquents and their inclusion in a moral dilemma discussion group. *Psychological Reports* 39, 1075–80.

Friedman, W. J., Robinson, A. B. and Friedman, B. (1987) Sex differences in moral judgments? A test of Gilligan's theory. *Psychology of Women Quarterly* 11, 37–46.

Gardner, E. M. (1983) *Moral Education for the Emotionally Disturbed Early Adolescent*. Lexington, Massachusetts: Lexington Books, D.C. Heath and Co.

Gibbs, J., Arnold, K., Ahlborn, H. and Cheesman, F. (1984) Facilitation of socio-moral reasoning in delinquents. *Journal of Consulting and Clinical Psychology* 1, 37–45.

Glueck, E. T. (1966) Identification of potential delinquents at 2–3 years of age. *The International Journal of Social Psychiatry* 12, 5–6.

Henggeler, S. W. (1989) *Delinquency in Adolescence*. Newbury Park, California: Sage Publications.

Hersh, R. H., Miller, J. P. and Fielding, G. D. (1980) *Models of Moral Education: An Appraisal*. New York: Longman, Inc.

Jurkovic, G. (1980) The juvenile delinquent as a moral philosopher: A struc-tural–developmental perspective. *Psychological Bulletin* 88, 709–27.

Kaestle, C. F. (1984) Moral education and common schools in America: A historian's view. *Journal of Moral Education* 13, 101–11.

Kohlberg, L. (1976) Moral stages and moralization: The cognitive develop-mental approach. In T. Lickona (ed.), *Moral Development and Behavior: Theory, Research, and Social Issues* (pp. 31–53). New York: Holt, Rinehart, and Winston.

Krebs, D. L., Vermeulen, S. C., Denton, K. L. and Carpendale, J. I. (1994) Gender and perspective differences in moral judgment and moral orienta-tion. *Journal of Moral Education* 23, 17–26.

Kuhmerker, L. (1973) We don't call it moral education: American children learn about values. *Journal of Moral Education* 3, 359–65.

Laub, J. H., Sampson, R. J., Corbett, R. P., Jr. and Smith, J. S. (1995) The public policy implications of a life-course perspective on crime. In H. Barlow (ed.), *Crime and Public Policy: Putting Theory to Work* (pp. 91–106). Boulder, Colorado: Westview Press.

Launay, G. (1987) Victim–offender conciliation. In B. J. McGurk, D. M. Thornton and M. Williams (eds.), *Applying Psychology to Imprisonment: Theory and Practice* (pp. 273–302). London: HMSO.

Lee, M. and Prentice, N. (1988) Interrelations of empathy, cognition, and moral reasoning with dimensions of juvenile delinquency. *Journal of Abnormal Child Psychology* 16, 127–39.

Leitenberg, H. (1987) Primary prevention and delinquency. In J. D. Burchard and S. N. Burchard (eds.), *Prevention of Delinquent Behavior* (pp. 312–30). Newbury Park, California: Sage.

Lickona, T. (1976) Critical issues in the study of moral development and behavior. In T. Lickona (ed.), *Moral Development and Behavior: Theory, Research, and Social Issues* (pp. 3–27). New York: Holt, Rinehart, and Winston.

Locke, D. (1983) Doing what comes morally: The relation between behavior and stages of moral reasoning. *Human Development* 26, 11–25.

Maguire, K. and Pastore, A. (eds.) (1996) *Sourcebook of Criminal Justice Statistics-1995*. Bureau of Justice Statistics, US Department of Justice. Washington, DC: USGPO.

Nelson, J. R., Smith, D. J. and Dodd, J. (1990) The moral reasoning of juve-nile delinquents: A meta-analysis. *Journal of Abnormal Child Psychology* 18, 231–9.

Niles, W. J. (1986) Effects of a moral development discussion group on delin-quent and predelinquent boys. *Journal of Counseling Psychology* 33, 45–51.

Prentice, N. (1972) The influence of live and symbolic modeling on promot-ing moral judgment of adolescent delinquents. *Journal of Abnormal Psychology* 80, 157–61.

Raine, A. (1993) *The Psychopathology of Crime*. San Diego: Academic Press.

Rosenkoetter, L., Landman, S. and Mazak, S. (1980) Use of moral discus-sion as an intervention with delinquents. *Psychological Reports* 46, 91–4.

Rowe, D. and Newton, J. (1994) *You, Me, Us!* London: The Home Office.

Sampson, R. J. and Laub, J. H. (1993) *Crime in the Making: Pathways and Turning Points Through Life*. Cambridge: Harvard University Press.

Schlaefli, A., Rest, J. and Thoma, S. J. (1985) Does moral education improve moral judgment? A meta-analysis of intervention studies using the Defining Issues Test. *Review of Educational Research* 55, 319–52.

Schorr, L. B. (1988) *Within Our Reach*. New York: Doubleday.

Smetana, J. G. (1990) Morality and conduct disorders. In M. Lewis and S. M. Miller (eds.), *Handbook of Developmental Psychopathology* (pp. 157–79). New York: Plenum Press.

Smith, L. A. (1978) *Moral Education* (Report of a One-Day Conference by the School of Education, Goldsmith's College in Conjunction with the Goldsmith's College Association). London: Goldsmith's College.

Snarey, J. R. (1985) Cross-cultural universality of social-moral development: A critical review of Kohlbergian research. *Psychological Bulletin* 97, 202–32.

Stouthamer-Loeber, M. and Loeber, R. (1988) The use of prediction data in understanding delinquency. *Behavioral Sciences and the Law* 6, 333–54.

Thornton, D. M. (1987) Moral development theory. In B. J. McGurk, D. M. Thornton and M. Williams (eds.), *Applying Psychology to Imprisonment: Theory and Practice* (pp. 129–50). London: HMSO.

Walker, L. J. (1984) Sex differences in the development of moral reasoning: A critical review. *Child Development* 55, 677–91.

——. (1986) Sex differences in the development of moral reasoning: A rejoinder to Baumrind. *Child Development* 57, 522–6.

Worrall, A. (1995) Troublesome young women. *Criminal Justice Matters* 19, 6–7.

Afterword: How Can Young Men Learn Virtue?

Mary Tuck

'Treatment' people are seen as soft, wimpy lefties who, when a kid has committed a crime, think he just needs some tender loving care and an anger management course to be put back on track. 'Punishment' people are thought to be somewhere to the right of Attila the Hun, believing that when a kid misbehaves or breaks the criminal law, what he really needs is a good birching or a period of several years in an austere prison. We must get beyond 'treatment' and 'punishment'; they represent a simplistic dichotomy in which those of us involved with criminal justice issues must not become trapped. We need a new way of dealing with juvenile crime, and somehow, most of us seem to think, this new thinking is going to be bound up with ideas of community – of man as a social animal.

But how can we define such a new path? I would like to turn the usual question upside-down, and ask not 'How can we stop people from being bad?' but 'How can we help people to become good?'. The source to which I turn to answer this question is the thought of Aristotle, especially as revived in the work of Alasdair McIntyre.

Aristotle offers a theory of how men learn the virtues, and by the virtues he did not mean some arbitrary rules of conventional morality. Aristotle's morality is something very different to our post-Kantian, post-Enlightenment morality. He taught that habits of virtue arise through joint human practices, joint human activity. In any society men need to learn to 'act well' in certain very practical ways. 'Acting well' means learning to do something properly, as it demands to be done. In ancient societies men had to learn to be good potters, good warriors, good housekeepers, or good farmers. In modern society, then, 'acting well' means being a good computer programmer or good nurse or good driver, or even a good petrol-pump hand or fast-food cook.

You may say this practical sort of 'acting well' isn't at all what is commonly thought of as a moral sense. But the point is that to learn to 'act well' in these very specific, practical matters requires men to learn from, and build upon, the skills of others. Furthermore, to learn from others requires certain internal dispositions, such as humility, perseverance, honesty, respect, and the courage to try and try again. We need to learn these dispositions if we are to 'act well' in any ordinary or extraordinary endeavor. It is these necessary internal dispositions, then, which are collectively known as the virtues.

If a society is to succeed, it needs to encourage these virtues, otherwise joint social action will not flourish. Having learned the virtues in this sense is to become what is called a 'good man'. We learn to become good men by engaging in collaborative activities. But there will always be those who fail to learn. How does society deal with them? In the first instance, society must stop them from harming the joint life of the community. Thus it is necessary for any society to proscribe those actions which make joint social projects difficult or impossible, for at least some of the time in at least some places. Such actions as the taking of innocent life, theft, perjury, or betrayal must be forbidden. To proscribe such actions is the function of criminal law.

But note that the criminal law alone cannot teach men the virtues. That is not its function. As Thomas Aquinas, himself a good Aristotelian, remarked, 'Training that operates through fear of punishment is the kind of training that law imposes'. Though the criminal law is necessary for social protection, it is not in itself enough to sustain a good society.

Where does such a theory lead us in the matter of juvenile crime? Doesn't this fit very well with what we know about the causes of delinquency? We know what kind of young man commits most of the crime in our society. Characteristically he comes from a home marked by conflict (a third of British prisoners have been in state childcare), he comes from the poorer areas of our inner cities and has probably grown up in an anonymous tower block with such a shifting population that it is hard for him to know any neighbors. He will have attended a large school where few in authority learned his name, will have truanted from school by the age of 12, will have no qualifications and will never be able to get a steady job. Characteristically he is a young man, as the phrase goes, 'on the margins of society'. He has never learned what I have called 'joint practices'. He has grown up in our cities like a wolf-child, unsocialized, unsupported, and uncivilized. Naturally, he has never learned the virtues.

But, because human beings are marvelous and will not or cannot live alone, the delinquent will join the only social group open to him – a gang of similar youth on the street. He joins the modern version of the warrior band, in which he begins to learn some joint practices, such as nicking car radios or stealing from electric meters. In this way he begins to develop some rudiments of the virtues, like loyalty to his mates, patience, and ingenuity. Unfortunately, the group he has joined is against society at large, and excludes the ordinary citizen, the old lady he robs or the working man whose car he vandalizes. So his behavior has to be proscribed and forbidden, and the sooner and more efficiently the better. He needs to be stopped in his tracks, but he also needs to learn the virtues. This is our dual task.

How might this be managed? First, he needs to be caught soon, early in his criminal career. That requires efficient policing, targeted to where the crime is happening. Current clear-up rates in the UK and US are far too low. We could do better, even in our anonymous cities, if the police were given the computers and information aids they needed. Research on victimization patterns has consistently shown that most crime happens to those to whom it has happened already. Protect the victims better, and you will catch more criminals.

Second, the delinquent youth needs to be punished quickly and efficiently. This means limiting his freedom and autonomy, either for part of his time under the supervision of the probation service or for all the time in prison. The severity of the punishment is far less important than its certainty and speed. This result, well known to economists and educators, seems to be too often forgotten in matters of crime. In the US, for example, crime rates across the states are more sensitive to certainty of arrest than to sentence length once caught.

Third, while the offender is being punished we must try to train him in the virtues, and this means offering him the opportunity of joint activity with others, of learning a real skill or social joint practice. Learning things with others does not have to be undertaken with a specific future job in mind. But giving him the experience of having to learn a skill from, and with, others develops virtue.

Finally, when his due punishment is over, every effort must be made to re-insert him into some positive social grouping where he can find lawful ways of doing useful things with fellow men. Most crime is committed by people who have already been through the criminal justice system. It is minimal, sensible crime prevention to offer alternative paths to those released from prisons and jails, or other types of criminal justice supervision.

All these prescriptions may seem, and even are, totally obvious. But we don't follow them, do we? This is because public debate about crime is hung up on the tiresome division between treatment versus punishment, as if we could only follow one path or the other. One means of combining both goals is through the use of probation sentences. Probation can offer many tough and demanding punishments without providing residential accommodation. Prison and the non-custodial penalties offered through probation should be seen not as opposites, but alternatives along a continuum. In the UK I would like to see them both administered jointly under a 'National Corrections Service'. Prison is necessary if and when an offender needs to be kept out of the community temporarily because of the danger he presents. When he is let out, he needs to be under the supervision of the probation service. Attendance at probation disposals must be rigidly enforced, and prison applied as the sanction when youngsters violate their probation terms. Still, the experiences of common learning and common training in joint practices are almost always more successfully provided in the community by the probation service. To attend the hours required in itself cultivates discipline and represents a type of training in the virtues. Such training is much more difficult to achieve in a prison setting, where prisoners are without autonomy.

Everything I have mentioned so far is about how to treat the offender after he has been caught. The more important task is to prevent the young men turning to crime in the first place. This will require, at a minimum, setting up programs in our inner cities such that the young men have something to do, so that they can learn joint skills from others and develop virtue. We need to offer ways of learning joint practices before youngsters become entangled in a life of crime. Would this be so difficult? It would certainly be easier in the UK than in the racially segregated wastelands of many US cities. The Victorians accomplished it through boys' clubs and settlements. We need to re-invent this type of joint activity for our isolated and deprived youth. We need clubs and buildings with a few tools and experts on hand where youngsters can go and mend their own bicycles, make their own music, and renovate household machines. This would allow those who would otherwise fall into a gang and a delinquent lifestyle to acquire skills and patience, to join a community they never before had the chance to join. In addition to these types of program in the community, we also need to fund the probation service adequately so that it can fulfil its responsibilities by offering such rehabilitating programs in addition to supervision.

But, if my American friends will forgive me saying so, what we do not need is to follow the US experience of mass imprisonment. Indeed, even discounting the proliferation of guns in the US, American youth are much more violent than their British counterparts; and so imprisonment is needed more in the US than in the UK. Still, I think the rocketing rates of juvenile violence in America are linked somehow with the brutalizing experiences many suffer in overcrowded jails and prisons. Though similar in important ways, our two countries are very different in others. We have a tradition in Britain and America of joint social action. However, in Britain we do think the state has a role to play in arranging things so that men have opportunities to do good. We have in Britain, in short, a greater sense of community and social solidarity, even in the most deprived and disturbed parts of our cities, compared to the US. These are assets we must build upon as we march into the future. Rather than blindly building more prisons, let both countries reconsider the importance of teaching young men virtue. But we cannot stop there. To achieve a better society, we cannot rest with just a consideration of such ideas, but must act upon them as well.

Index